Biog.   66-1935
Roosevelt
    Judson, Clara
    Theodore, Roosevelt

DATE DUE			

Harford Day School

Bel Air, Maryland

Even as a sickly boy, Theodore Roosevelt had interesting adventures and traveled to fascinating faraway places. The story of his courageous fight for health, his life as a hunter and rancher, and his service to his city, state, and country is thrilling to read.

It was still the Wild West in those days . . . a land of vast silent spaces, of lonely rivers, and of plains where the wild game stared at the passing horseman. It was a land of scattered ranches, of herds of long-horned cattle, and of reckless riders who unmoved looked in the eyes of life or of death. In that land we led a free and hardy life, with horse and with rifle. . . . We knew toil and hardship and hunger and thirst; and we saw men die violent deaths as they worked among the horses and cattle, or fought in evil feuds with one another; but we felt the beat of hardy life in our veins, and ours was the glory of work and the joy of living.

THEODORE ROOSEVELT

(Autobiography)

Theodore Roosevelt

Fighting Patriot

by Clara Ingram Judson

PENCIL DRAWINGS BY

Lorence F. Bjorklund

Follett Publishing Company

CHICAGO

Author's Foreword

Three biographies already published in this group tell the stories of Washington, Jefferson, and Lincoln, men long separated from us in time. As I thought over the many heroes who have helped in man's journey toward freedom, I had a desire to write about someone who lived nearer to our own day, our problems, our ways. So I took a bird's eye view of American history — and a vacation, my first visit to the great Southwest.

There I saw the great transformation of vast deserts brought about by conservation and irrigation begun early in our own century. Later, studying the history of conservation in our country, I learned that this opening of arid land and rescue of forests sprang largely from the work of one man. A man who was neither forester nor farmer, but who loved the out-of-doors. A man who used his peculiar mixture of patriotism and the publicist's skill to interest Americans in the conservation of their natural resources. This man was our twenty-sixth president, Theodore Roosevelt.

Because of his vigor, his democratic ideals, and his public service, his personality was impressed on more than a generation of American youth. Today he is taking his place with other great Americans — as on Mount Rushmore. His beloved home, Sagamore Hill, is now a national shrine, visited along with Mount Vernon, Monticello, and New Salem. A new exhibit of his specimens is to open this autumn in the American Museum of Natural History in New York.

In this war-torn world, we look back and see how Theodore Roosevelt worked for peace — not peace of appeasement or of harsh victory, but peace with justice. He had the gift of inspiring others to serve their country. He and his sons risked their lives in battle; and three died in the service of their country, Quentin, Theodore Junior, and Kermit. Today we know that he should be followed not only in war, but in his long battle for honest government and for justice for all people.

Anyone who cares enough can serve his country as Theodore Roosevelt did, in ward and city, in state and nation. Faraway foes may threaten us, but the greatest danger to a free nation is the indifference and apathy of its citizens. Today and always we need fighting patriots.

As with my other biographies, many people have given me kind and competent help in the research. I am indebted to Theodore Roosevelt's daughter Ethel, Mrs. Richard Derby, for facts and inspiration; to Miss Mae V. Manning, Curator of the Theodore Roosevelt Museum in Roosevelt's birthplace, 28 East 20th Street, New York City, for patiently answering questions and for reading my manuscript; to Mr. Thomas Little, who is in charge of the Theodore Roosevelt Collection at Harvard College Library; and to my daughter Alice, Mrs. Gordon Canning, for my discovery of the Southwest.

Mr. Waldo L. Schmitt, Head Curator, Department of Zoology, Smithsonian Institution, Washington, D. C.; Mrs. Josephine Kimball and Mr. William A. Burns of the American Museum of Natural History in New York City informed me about the present availability of many of the Roosevelt trophies — rhinoceroses, antelopes, buffaloes, Egyptian and American birds. Mrs. Kimball has responsibility for the permanent Theodore Roosevelt exhibit soon to be opened in the American Museum of Natural History. Charles Scribner's Sons gave permission to quote the portion of the letter on page 36. The quotation from the *Autobiography* opposite the frontispiece is used by permission of the publishers, copyright 1913 by Charles Scribner's Sons, 1941 by Edith K. Carow Roosevelt. And as always, Miss Louise Borchelt and Miss Florence Davison of the Evanston Public Library gave invaluable help. To these and many others, I am grateful.

C. I. J.

Evanston, Illinois
July 27, 1953

Theodore Roosevelt Fighting Patriot

28 East Twentieth Street

A Sunday hush lay upon the Roosevelt home in New York City. Sounds of cooking and laying the table for dinner were muffled by nearby doors, tightly closed. Even the three restless children who waited at the top of a handsome stairway were quiet, listening, as they peered into the dim front hall below.

"Is it time for him, Teedie?" the little girl asked the older of her two brothers.

"Yes. It's time." Elliott spoke quickly before his brother could reply. "I looked at the clock. Church is over."

"*Listen!*" Theodore raised his hand imperiously. "Those are our horses. Now we may go down."

Starched blouses and scratchy collars, so annoying a moment before, were forgotten as Corinne, Elliott, and Theodore plunged down the long stairs. The butler sprang to open the heavy door, and the three raced down more steps to throw themselves upon Mr. Theodore Roosevelt as he stepped from his carriage.

"Will you take us driving *now*, Father?" Theodore junior cried, panting.

"You promised you would if the day was fine," said Elliott.

"Please, Father!" Corinne implored, clinging to his hand.

"You do not need to *beg*," Mr. Roosevelt laughed at their eagerness as he turned to help Mrs. Roosevelt and his older daughter Anna from the carriage. "Of course we shall drive — this is a wonderful day and I need air after that long sermon. How are you, Teedie, better?" He looked keenly at the thin, worn face of his older son. A boy of eight should not have those dark shadows under his eyes, nor that patient, haggard look that came after nights of pain. But what to do? No one seemed to know.

"I'm fine, Father," Theodore was saying, gaily. "I can drive as long as you will take us." He grinned up at the tall man. Apparently the pain and misery of the night were forgotten.

"That's my boy!" Mr. Roosevelt's eyes sparkled with approval, though he could not forget the lad's cruel, gasping struggle to breathe. "When an attack is over, forget it. Get me my driving gloves, Ellie, and we'll be off." He turned to his wife. "Will you go with us, my dear?"

"You go too fast for me," Mrs. Roosevelt declined, smiling. "Anna must rest, and I have duties. Dinner will be ready in an hour — I shall expect you."

"Let me take your coat, my dear," Mr. Roosevelt said as he followed her up the steps. The children waited patiently while their father tenderly took off her wrap and handed it to the waiting butler. This ritual of care for their mother always vaguely pleased them, even when it made them wait.

Meanwhile the groom had driven off with the team and the stately carriage used for church attendance. He returned with the trap, a kind of phaeton, roomy and high, and the spike-team, a leader horse hitched in front of a pair. These three horses were handsome creatures; the leader tossed his head, eager to be off.

Mr. Roosevelt put on the gloves Elliott handed him and set Corinne on the high seat. While the two boys climbed up beside her, he took the reins from the groom and swung himself up to the driver's place.

"Hold tight, now," he warned. "We're off!"

The horses dashed away, rounded the corner, the trap poised precariously as they made the turn into Fifth Avenue. The children clutched hats, the seat arm, and each other, and laughed with glee. This noontime drive was the high spot of the whole week. No one in all New York drove with more daring, wove in and out of traffic with more skill, than Theodore Roosevelt, the well known banker and merchant.

But the ride ended promptly. Nothing must delay Sunday dinner.

Reluctantly, the children took off their wraps and filed into the dining room. They had no love for that place. It was a somber room; the chairs were too high for comfort and were covered with haircloth that scratched. They preferred the nursery where most of their meals were served. The pleasure of Sunday dinner was their father's company. They liked the sound of his deep voice as he talked with his wife and her

mother and sister. They thrilled when his frequent smile showed he noticed them. And the dinner was good.

This house on East Twentieth Street was a lively place; its formalities were merely the usual customs of the late 1860's among the people the Roosevelts knew in New York City.

The tall narrow building was set between other houses of similar design. The service entrance below the sidewalk level was hidden by imposing steps to the front door. The hall led to handsomely furnished parlor, library, and dining room. On the next floor, Mr. and Mrs. Roosevelt's room and the adjoining nursery were the center of daytime living. Other family rooms were on the third floor; servants' quarters and attic were on the topmost floor.

The head of this household was a vigorous man of Welsh, Holland-Dutch, and Scotch-Irish descent. The mother was a beautiful and gracious Southern lady from Georgia.

An aunt, uncle, and several cousins lived next door and were especially admired by Theodore and his sisters because they kept a variety of pets. Pheasants, peacocks, and modest peahens strode up and down the narrow back yard, and a pet monkey was allowed to climb over back stairs and porches.

These animals, and others Theodore learned of in books, were used as characters in long, imagined tales which he told to Elliott and Corinne. Sometimes after a bad night, he sat propped up with pillows and told them "what happened next."

His poor health prevented Theodore from going to school, so his mother's sister, Aunt Anna Bulloch, taught him for an hour each morning. He was an avid reader and was allowed to read whatever he chose from the library downstairs. For hours at a time, he would sit curled up on the sofa, his face close to the printed page, entranced. He liked nature stories and adventure and tales about animals.

This wide reading gave him an unusual vocabulary. And as Theodore's ill health prevented play with children, he used this vocabulary and the correct English his parents spoke. Such formal talk would have sounded odd to most Americans in the 1860's; but it was natural for him.

Soon after that Sunday ride the Roosevelt family packed up, closed the city house, and went to the country for the summer. The children's chatter on the train was about the fun of previous summers and plans for the new season.

"I shall run to the stable and see if General Grant has grown," Theodore announced.

"Ponies don't grow," his sister Anna said. "General Grant will be the same as last year."

"I shall ride him by myself this year, Father," Theodore announced, hopefully. "And I shall get a rabbit the first day."

"I like rabbits better than mice," Corinne said.

"I shall collect mice, too," Theodore added. "This year I shall make a collection in the interest of science."

Anna laughed. "You read that, Teedie, you never thought that up yourself. It would be better if you used your eyes to see where you were going. Remember last — "

"Gather up your things, children," Mrs. Roosevelt interrupted. "We are almost there now."

The menagerie grew to be very large that summer — coons,

membering it. "We can move the piles of magazines. . . ."

"I could put magazines on the floor here, Mother," Theodore said, hopefully. "I'm the one who reads them."

"Not on the floor, Son; we can bring down the set of open shelves in the attic. Be patient, Teedie. Sort your things while I have the shelves washed. . . ."

"And I may keep everything, Mother?"

"Dear me, NO!" Mrs. Roosevelt exclaimed, "Keep only the stuff that does not smell."

"This is not 'stuff', Mother," Theodore said with dignity. "These are scientific specimens. But I shall save only the choicest."

"Mind you do that." His mother hurried away from the hateful odors to call for the help of maid and houseman. Behind her, Theodore began sorting, a painful task.

Finally the bookcase in the hall was full. Theodore printed a sign and posted it at the top:

ROOSEVELT MUSEUM OF NATURAL HISTORY

And he went around with the key to the case in his pocket, lest his mother, in a housewifely moment, should throw out his treasures.

Even though the case was full, Theodore kept alert for new specimens. Some time later his search was rewarded. He was walking alone, up Broadway, amusing himself by peering into windows, his nose against the panes, or inspecting counters in the open air markets. Suddenly he almost poked his face into a noisome, moist fur spread on a plank.

"What is that?" he asked, as he drew back, startled.

"A dead seal," the merchant said casually.

"A seal!" Theodore was enchanted. The word, the smell, seemed to bring adventure to commonplace Broadway. "Where from?"

"The harbor. Someone caught it."

"Oh, please, sir, may I study it? I never saw a seal before."

The man turned to look at him. "Oh, you're a Roosevelt. Study all you like, it stinks well."

Theodore dashed home for a pencil, note paper, and the only measure he could find, a wooden footrule, awkward for his need. He ran all the way back, eager to get at the project before the merchant changed his mind. He measured and estimated and set down rows of figures which seemed to him priceless discoveries of science. The next day and the next he was back to hunt new facts to write down.

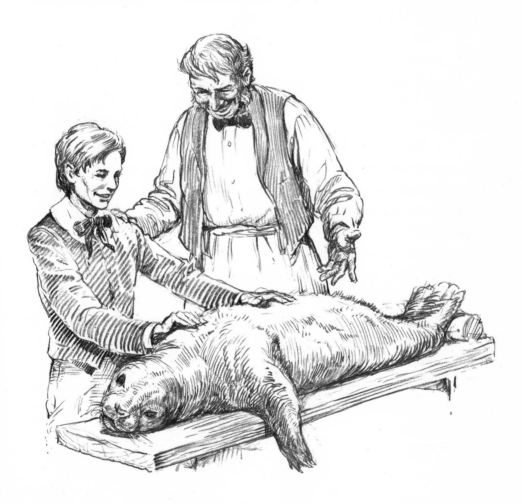

Alas! A day came when customers insisted that the dead seal must go — permanently. Theodore begged so hard for the bony skull that the merchant let him take it home. Somehow he contrived to find a place for it in the museum. He hoped it would be safe there.

The early years of young Theodore's life were a constant struggle for health. That same decade was a difficult period for the country he lived in, too.

When Theodore was born, October 27, 1858, Abraham Lincoln was closing his debates with Stephen A. Douglas, out in Illinois. On the lad's third birthday, Lincoln was president and the nation was engaged in a terrible civil war.

Mr. Roosevelt was devoted to Lincoln and to the ideal of the Union, but because his wife was a Southerner he chose to do civilian war work rather than military. He planned and put through a bill for soldiers' allotments, a new idea then; he visited the front lines to explain to soldiers how they could order part of their pay sent to families at home. He worked for relief and a War-Claim Association and skillfully publicized these and other good causes.

The children missed their father when he was in Washington and at the front. They were happy when the war ended and he could stay at home. He again attended to his business and to the charitable work he loved. The Roosevelts were not interested in politics. Hospitals, newsboys' lodgings, aid for immigrants, and help for needy persons that they chanced to know seemed more important.

Post-war years were happy except for concern about Theodore's health. The family spent the summer vacation in a new place, but the lad grew worse. The parents were deeply discouraged.

Then suddenly Mr. Roosevelt was cheerful. Workmen invaded the house, and the nursery door was locked. But not a word would he tell the mystified children.

"Mayn't we *see*, Father?" Elliott begged. "It's our nursery."

Mr. Roosevelt grinned and shook his head.

"No, you may not see. You are not even to peek. If you do —— " The implied threat cowed Elliott. He kept at a respectful distance. But curiosity grew steadily.

Struggle for Health

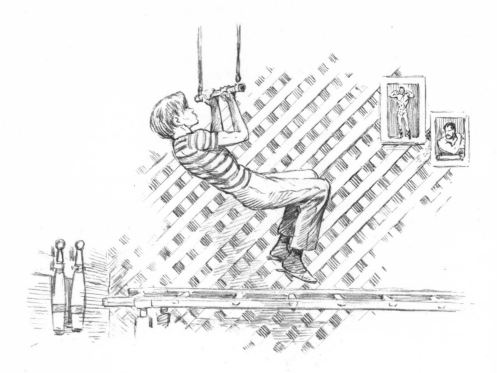

The day came when workmen packed their tools and departed; the house seemed strangely quiet. And that evening Mr. Roosevelt invited Theodore into the library.

"Mayn't Connie and I come, too?" Elliott asked.

"Later. I shall talk to Teedie first." He closed the door and drew Theodore down beside him on the haircloth sofa.

"The time has come, my son, to take positive action about your health. You have a good mind in a sickly body. Doctors seem unable to cure you, so I am giving you a chance to help yourself. You can make yourself strong and perhaps in this way overcome your great disability."

Theodore blinked at his vigorous father, trying to understand.

"You will need courage and determination," Mr. Roosevelt went on. "But if you are diligent I think you can become a strong, sturdy lad."

"Strong. Sturdy." Theodore whispered the words. They had the sound of magic. "You mean I am to strive daily like the knights of old?" His face was radiant.

"Exactly!" Mr. Roosevelt patted his son's shoulder. "I knew you would get my idea. Nothing ails your brains, but you must remake your body. Your jousting field is in this house."

"Here!" Theodore felt deflated. The dim, austere library had no suggestion of the medieval jousting field, gay with banners, his imagination had conjured up.

"Yes. Come upstairs, and I shall show you."

He grabbed Theodore's hand, hurried across the room, and opened the door. Elliott and Corinne fell into the library; they had been taking turns at the keyhole. Laughing, the four dashed up the stairs. At the nursery door, Mr. Roosevelt paused, selected a key from his silver ring and handed it to Theodore.

"This is your surprise, Teedie," he said. "You open it."

Impressed with this privilege, Theodore turned the key and opened the door. The nursery was as always except for a pair of wooden steps set by the far window. The children dashed to climb these and peer outside.

The space south of the nursery had been a kind of porch, little used. Now it was partly enclosed and furnished as a gymnasium. Horizontal bars were built in; a trapeze swung above their heads. Dumbbells were in a rack and Indian clubs stood in a corner near a sturdy ladder, set crosswise.

"This is Theodore's room," Mr. Roosevelt announced impressively. "Here he will make himself a strong, sturdy boy."

Corinne stared. Elliott laughed.

"Will he know how?" Corinne asked, frowning at Elliott.

"Yes. I shall show him. And you two are not to tease him or entice him away for stories."

"I'll let them come here," Theodore said grandly.

"Thanks, Teedie," Elliott said, a bit awed.

"Come any time," Theodore added. The sensation of giving a favor was delightful. "Just help yourselves."

Mr. Roosevelt picked up a pair of dumbbells and began swinging them. "One, two, three, four," he said briskly. "Up, two; down, four. See how it goes, Son? Do only eight counts at first; then rest." He set the things in the rack, picked up Indian clubs and swung those.

"Do ten minutes; then later, another ten. Afternoons do twice fifteen minutes. Mustn't get stiff. Steady faithful exercise will bring strength." This last was spoken half to himself, hopefully. They had tried so many things, and failed.

Theodore did the exercises faithfully. Dumbbells, bars, trapeze — he used all the paraphernalia of a proper gymnasium of the late sixties.

"Aren't you sick of it?" Elliott asked a month later.

"Yes," Theodore admitted. "But I can't disappoint Father. Feel my arm. I think I have more muscle already."

"Oh, you and your muscle! I think the whole thing is silly." Elliott slid down the bannisters and left for play.

Alone, Theodore looked longingly toward the nursery. How he would love to curl up with a book! But he began counting, "One, two, bend right . . ." After a few weeks he could exercise for half an hour. That was some progress.

His father was the impatient one. He put Theodore in a nearby school. But boys teased the lad with the pipestem legs. "You're so dumb you can't do the problems on the board!" they twitted him. The day Theodore came home with a bloody face he was taken out of school and a tutor hired for him.

The next summer the Roosevelts again went to a new country place in the hope of helping Theodore. He was able to walk a mile and climb a small hill; the gymnasium had helped. But asthma came back in the nights, terrible attacks.

At breakfast some time later Mr. Roosevelt ate absently. Suddenly he exclaimed, "We must do something for Teedie! He slept less than an hour last night. I walked the floor with him. Then I propped him up with pillows and read till dawn."

"But what can we do?" Mrs. Roosevelt asked anxiously. Anna, Corinne, and Elliott ate their oatmeal silently. Some one was always fussing about Teedie, his health, his clumsiness, his collections.

"I have decided that we should go to another climate," Mr. Roosevelt announced with more assurance than he felt. "I think we should travel a year in Europe."

"And not go to school?" Elliott asked quickly, hardly daring to credit such bliss.

"We could visit my brothers," Mrs. Roosevelt remarked.

"What would *we* do?" Corinne asked.

"Oh, visit churches and art galleries, and see sights," the father replied vaguely. "Travel is educational."

The children's interest faded. When they were excused

they dashed upstairs. Maybe Theodore was awake and would finish yesterday's story. Even when ill, he could make up a fascinating tale.

The idea of travel pleased Mr. Roosevelt. In May of the year 1869, when Theodore was ten and a half, they left New York on the S. S. *Scotia,* a paddle-wheel ship that intrigued the children. With Theodore leading, they explored everywhere; stumbling over rope, hatches, and people, until beyond the harbor a high wind came up and all were violently seasick.

Theodore recovered first and began to make friends. His method was direct. He asked questions of everyone he saw; if the answer showed knowledge of natural history, he questioned further. If not, he went on to someone else.

After the search he chose for his best friend an odd little man who had a wide knowledge of birds and beasts. By the time Corinne and Elliott had recovered from rough seas Theodore had lost all interest in exploring and games. He wrote the daily letters his father required; and the rest of each day he sat on a pile of rope in the lee of a lifeboat, talking science with his new friend.

The Roosevelts landed at Liverpool and went at once to visit Mrs. Roosevelt's brothers. Uncle Jimmy and Uncle Irvine Bulloch delighted the children with war tales.

"Your father was a good friend of Abraham Lincoln," Uncle Jimmy remarked, remembering his manners to Yankees.

"I remember Abraham Lincoln," Theodore shouted.

"You couldn't," Uncle was amazed. "You never saw him."

"But I remember!" Theodore insisted. "We saw from

Grandfather's window — on 14th Street. The lamp-posts had black cloth over them. Houses had black streamers. The procession moved slowly; the music went boom — boom — boom, like that." He slid from his chair and marched with dignity across the room as the children stared at him.

"He means Lincoln's funeral!" Uncle Irvine exclaimed. "There was a parade in New York — "

"Yes, that's what I mean," Theodore insisted. "I saw it from Grandfather's window. It was so long that Grandfather thought I would be tired watching. But I wasn't."

"I was there, too?" Corinne said doubtfully.

"You were only four, Connie. And Ellie was two — just a baby. I remember well."

"You do indeed," Uncle Irvine agreed, recovering from his surprise. "Now let Jimmy tell you about when we blocked the Yanks. Jimmy was an admiral in the Confederate Navy."

"Uncle Irvine should tell his tale," Jimmy said modestly. "He was the midshipman who stayed to fire the last shot aboard the *Alabama* in the fight with the S.S. *Kearsarge*."

"What happened then?" Elliott asked.

"The *Alabama* sank. Your uncle grabbed a plank and swam around till he was rescued. Those Yanks . . ." The tales went on for hours. The children never seemed to weary.

After the Liverpool visit, the Roosevelts began touring. Mornings were for letters; the children had to write accounts of all they saw to send relatives and friends. Most of Corinne's letters went to her chum, Edith Carow, whom she sadly missed. Afternoons they visited churches, art galleries and famous places.

"The galleries are all alike," Theodore remarked, as they left a notable one, "just full of pictures."

"Do we have to see another cathedral today?" Elliott inquired dolefully. His mother laughed and shook her head.

"Will we be home for Teedie's birthday?" Corinne asked.

"Dear me, no! Let's see . . . October 27th. We'll be in

Austria then, on the way to Rome." The children sighed.

"But we'll have a real birthday, anything you like, Teedie."

"I'd like to have breakfast in our rooms and me tell the waiter what we want to eat," Theodore said quickly. "And for dinner, I want you and Father to dress up in the clothes you wore for the party in London."

"That will be wonderful, Teedie," Corinne clapped her hands. "You always know exactly what you want."

On the journey to Austria, Theodore had a bad attack of asthma, but he recovered in time for the celebration he had planned.

After Rome, they went to Switzerland. There Theodore had the best time of the whole journey. He was able to take long walks and to climb a little. But the view that pleased the children most was their own home on Twentieth Street as they returned to it in the spring of 1870.

Summers, after this, were spent in the country near Riverdale, New York, on the Hudson River. Two southern cousins, Maude and John Elliott, came for long visits, and the five children were allowed freedom to roam about as they pleased.

Theodore, now twelve, continued the serious business of making a natural history collection. He advertised in the village paper for mice; ten cents for one field mouse; thirty-five cents for a healthy family. But alas! That very night asthma wrecked his plans. Early in the morning Mr. Roosevelt took the sick boy to the Berkshires, hoping he would get relief.

Anna, now a dignified teen-ager, was left to cope with the mice. The little creatures began arriving soon after the newspaper came out. By noon she had fifty-one; her own allowance was gone, and she had to beg money from her mother. Boxes covered with netting swarmed with lively creatures of various colors and ages. She posted a sign out in front, hoping to stop the influx of animals.

When Theodore returned, only slightly better for the journey, he found her feeding baby squirrels with a doll's nursing bottle.

"Some boys insisted that I buy these, Teedie," she said; "they're not mice. Your allowance for all summer is gone."

"Money! What do I care about *money!*" Theodore answered grandly. "You did right, Anna. I thank you. I'm glad someone in this family knows the importance of science. I'll finish the feeding. Then I'll skin and stuff the dead ones."

Anna gladly resigned as deputy-naturalist.

Theodore was undaunted by the number of animals. He spent mornings caring for them and afternoons hunting more. Often he returned bruised, scratched, and shabby.

"Teedie! You *must* watch where you are going!" his mother exclaimed often. "You are so awkward! Don't you ever *look?*"

"You always ask me that, Mother," Theodore said politely. "I do look. I did not see the stump that tore my pants, truly, Mother."

"You were thinking of something else, then. Now hurry and clean up for supper." Later she told her husband about this. "I don't know how to teach him to be careful," she said.

"Let him alone. He'll learn. Boys always get bumps," he replied. So the afternoon expeditions went on.

When the family arrived back in the city that autumn, there was the usual crisis about Theodore's treasures and the awful odors of dead creatures.

"Oh, Mother! Do let me learn to preserve them properly!" His mother stared at him, puzzled as to his meaning.

"I want to study taxidermy with Mr. Bell. I went to his shop often last spring. I think he would teach me."

"Your father will have to hear about this," she said.

The next morning at breakfast Mr. Roosevelt spoke of it.

"What's this about a Mr. Bell and his shop?"

"It's a wonderful place, Father!" Theodore's face lighted up. "Mr. Bell knows how to stuff birds, coons, mice — "

"And you want to learn, too?"

"Oh, I *do*, Father! Will you ask him to teach me?"

"Yes, we will see him now, before I go to the office."

In the tiny, cluttered shop, Theodore proudly introduced his father to Mr. Bell. After a few minute's talk, arrangements were made for lessons in taxidermy.

Now Theodore's days were filled with excitement. Mornings he had two hours with a tutor and a time in the gymnasium. Then he read till noon. He had his own way of choosing a book. He walked along the bookshelf and picked a volume at random. Flipping it open, he'd start reading. If, quite soon, he found something about an animal, he curled up in a big chair and went on reading it. If no animal appeared promptly, he put the book back on the shelf.

"Wonder why Father bought that one," he'd mutter, annoyed. Geography and history interested him only if he found

something about the wild life of a country.

The afternoon, though, was the best part of each day. In Mr. Bell's shop Theodore learned to skin a creature, treat the skin with arsenical soap, and painstakingly stuff and mount it. Soon his best trophies were in good condition, and he began to do Mr. Bell's. Winter had never seemed so short.

When they left for the country the following summer, Theodore was loaded down with books and taxidermy equipment. He knew he would have a wonderful summer. Nothing, not even scolding about his awkwardness, could bother him.

A New World

Alas! The summer had hardly begun when Theodore had one of his worst attacks of asthma and was sent off to the Maine woods. Sometimes he had been able to breathe better there. No one could go with him just then so he took the long trip by train and stagecoach alone.

All went well until the last lap of the journey when four husky youths boarded the stage. The sight of a skinny, pale boy amused them; they began to tease him, poking, pinching, tickling. He kicked and fought, but this entertained them the more, and they easily held him off so he could not touch them.

Fortunately the guide, Will Dow, was at the stage stop to meet him, and rescued the lad. But the experience rankled.

"What should I have done, Will?" Theodore asked, as they drove off to the camp.

"Nothing! You have no strength to fight. You've got to be strong. Walk and get good leg muscles. Box and develop your arms. Strength is the only thing bullies heed. You have to earn it yourself."

"Takes more than a gymnasium, Will?"

"Yes. But a man can be strong if he cares enough."

"Maybe Father will let me take boxing lessons in the fall." Theodore resolved to put this suggestion through.

In the woods, he improved and got back in time to share the big Fourth of July celebration with his family and their visitors. He wrote a letter to his aunt about that day:

"Dobb's Ferry, July 9th, 1872

"DEAR AUNTIE

We had the most splendid fun on the fourth of July. At eight o'clock we commenced with a discharge of three packs of firecrackers, which awoke most of the people. But we had only begun now, and during the remainder of the day six boxes of torpedoes and thirty-six packs of firecrackers kept the house in an exceedingly lively condition. That evening it rained which made us postpone the fireworks until the next evening, when they were had with great success, excepting the balloons which were an awful swindle. We boys assisted by firing roman candles, flowerpots and bengolas. We each got his fair share of burns."

After other bits of family news he signed the letter

"T D"

He liked the initials better than the nickname "Teedie" the
family persisted in using.

Theodore got along so well that later in that summer when
he was thirteen, his father gave him a gun. Mr. Roosevelt
had chosen a French gun, breech-loading, pin-fire and double
barrel type; a wise choice, he hoped, for a clumsy, absent-
minded boy. Theodore was ecstatic over his new possession.

"Now pay attention while I show you how the gun works.
There is no spring. If a cartridge sticks, you should be able to
get it out without killing yourself. But watch lest you tattoo
your face with unburned powder. Now run along with your
cousins and don't shoot toward the house! Remember?"

"Oh, I shall, Father! *Thank* you! I'll be careful!"

"That's one thing he never is," Mr. Roosevelt remarked to
his wife. "But he has to learn. Now look! Why didn't he go
around that bench instead of falling over it? I'll declare I don't
understand my own son!"

Theodore picked himself up and ran down the lawn.

"I've got a gun!" he shouted. "A real *gun!* Look!"

"New, too," Cousin John exclaimed, as neighbor boys gathered. 'I didn't know your father would give you one."

"Well, he did. He put in a cartridge. I'm going to shoot."

"Stand in line and take your turn then," John said.

Two boys shot. From their pleased exclamations Theodore
knew they had done well. When his turn came he held the gun
as they had, pointed toward the woods and pulled the trigger.

"You didn't even hit the target," Elliott scoffed.

"Didn't come within a mile — stupid!" Cousin John cried.

"How could I hit what isn't there?" Theodore demanded. "I aimed for the woods. When you set up a target, I'll hit it." He set his lips firmly, but he was shaking with anger.

"The target is too there!" Elliott shouted.

"It is *not!*" Theodore bristled. "I guess I know a target!"

"Look, Teedie," Cousin John thought this was going too far. "See that round thing down there? See colored rings?"

"No. I don't. You can't make me say I see what isn't there. I don't fool that easy."

"Will you admit it's there if we bump your nose on it?" One of the boys grabbed Theodore's shoulders and marched him down the lawn, the others close behind. They were five feet from their objective when Theodore stopped suddenly.

"Here's a white thing!" he exclaimed. He moved nearer. "It's got rings — white, yellow, blue. Is that what you were talking about, John?"

John drew back, astonished. The other boys stared.

"Your father must know about this," John said, concerned.

"Oh, don't tell him, John," Theodore begged. "He may take my gun away. I've seen the target. Now I can hit it."

"Nope. This is queer. Your father has to know."

Mr. Roosevelt saw the boys coming, Theodore trailing behind. What had happened now?

"Uncle Theodore," John began, glancing at his cousin, "he can't see the target. How can he learn to shoot?"

"Can't *see* the target — " Mr. Roosevelt was amazed.

"It's all right, Father," Theodore hurried to explain. "I've seen it now. Tell them not to move it, and I'll always know where to shoot." His father glanced upward.

"See that hawk, Son?" He pointed to a hawk, circling high.

"No, I don't, sir," Theodore said, looking up, directly at the hawk.

The boys stared at each other uneasily.

Mr. Roosevelt pulled out his watch. "There's a train in ten minutes. Lucky the carriage is here; hop in, Son. Ellie, tell Mother that I have taken Teedie to the city. I don't know when we shall return. Watch out, lads! We must hurry." Gravel splattered and hooves pounded as he drove off.

Hours passed before father and son came home.

"The oculist tells me that Theodore is near-sighted, very," Mr. Roosevelt told his wife. "Probably he was born that way."

"And we never knew!" she exclaimed reproachfully.

"The doctor cannot see why we never suspected."

"Would near-sightedness make him clumsy?" she asked.

"Yes, of course. He can see nothing until he is very close. It seems a marvel that he has not seriously injured himself. There'll be more tests. Those today seemed incredible."

Theodore made several trips before, finally, his father brought home his spectacles. The family were on the porch as Mr. Roosevelt jumped from the carriage and handed reins to the groom. Smiling, he opened a black spectacle case and took out steel-rimmed glasses with thick lenses.

"Come here, Son," he said. "Let's see how they fit."

Theodore squared his shoulders and stood before his father, face thrust forward, eyes tightly shut. Mr. Roosevelt slipped the case into his pocket and set the spectacles on his

son's nose, bows fitting neatly over the ears.

"Now look!" he said.

Theodore opened his eyes, turned slowly and inspected his family. Then he looked around the landscape, and up to the sky. Slowly a look of rapture lighted his face.

"Why, it's *beautiful!*" he exclaimed. "Look! The world is beautiful! I can see the flowers from here.

"There's your dog, Ellie, coming from the barn — why the barn's *big!* I never knew the barn was *big!*"

The children were silent, awed. His mother brushed away a tear.

"There's the carriage stone," Theodore went on. "I can see it from here!" His amazement shocked them.

Mr. Roosevelt patted his shoulder, too moved to speak.

"Glasses are wonderful, father!" Then he turned to his mother. "May I have a try at that target before supper?"

"Indeed you may, Teedie. We'll wait. Take your time." The boys ran toward the range, and this time Theodore did not fall over the bench.

Theodore learned to shoot very well, for a beginner, and after days of faithful practice his record compared well with the other boys'. His natural history collection improved, too, for now he could see small creatures he had missed before.

When the family returned to New York he started boxing lessons that the Maine guide had suggested, and he worked long hours in Mr. Bell's musty little shop getting his new trophies properly stuffed and mounted. This work, so important to Theodore, was progressing well when Mr. Roosevelt announced they were going to Europe.

"Again!" Elliott exclaimed.

"Must we really, Father?" Corinne asked.

"I cannot leave my collections, Father," Theodore said. "Truly I cannot now. You never seem to realize the importance of scientific study."

"This trip will not be like the other one," their father soothed them. "We shall go to Egypt. I hope to get a boat for a journey up the Nile River —"

"Can we hunt?" Theodore interrupted.

"Yes. We'll take our guns and do some shooting."

"Then I want to go." Theodore dashed to his room to begin sorting and packing taxidermy supplies.

This time the voyage was smooth and pleasant. Fourteen-year-old Theodore could see porpoises playing near and whales spouting in the distance. He found the ship and marine scenes enchanting now that he could see beyond his hands.

Visits in England were brief, and soon the family were in Alexandria, Egypt. There Mr. Roosevelt hired a *dehabeah,* a houseboat with sails, named *Aboo Erdan,* for a three-months voyage. While his father was making arrangements, Theodore poked about in shops; he chanced to find a handsome book about Egyptian birds. He bought it, for the scientific names intrigued him.

When they got aboard, Theodore promptly set up a taxidermy laboratory on the foredeck. Mornings, now, their nineteen-year-old sister Anna gave the children lessons, and they wrote letters and kept diaries. Afternoons, Theodore and his father went ashore to hunt. Usually they brought back birds or animals which Theodore identified with the help of his books and then prepared for shipping home. He found a use for his Latin as he toiled over the names of birds in the new book.

The *dehabeah* continued up the wide Nile. Sails were spread when a breeze blew; other days sailors walked on the riverbank dragging the boat with a heavy rope. Theodore worked hours on the foredeck while others took their ease under an awning at the stern. Occasionally American or European travelers on other boats came to call. One day, after they had been on the way for some time, a visitor remarked on the odd odor oboard.

"That's from my small son's taxidermy labors," Mr. Roosevelt apologized. "I'll show you where he works at his hobby."

Theodore did not pause on the arrival of the visitors. Nor did he appear to hear his father's explanations. But that evening he had a conference with his parent.

"I did not dispute you today, Father," he began, "but I think you should know that I am not a 'small boy' and that taxidermy is not a 'hobby.' I am making a scientific study of Egyptian birds. I shall give my specimens to American museums. My things are unique and will be welcomed."

Mr. Roosevelt gulped and eyed his son thoughtfully. He saw that the boy had changed, but so gradually that they had not noticed. He was taller; inches of his socks showed below trousers that had fitted in October. Hands, stained by chemicals, hung awkwardly below sleeves that were much too short. Face and bearing showed earnest purpose. The father had no idea that the boy's expectations would come true, but he did see that his son was developing and growing. This trip was proving successful.

"We must order a suit for Teedie," Mr. Roosevelt said to his wife, later. "His growth astonishes me!"

"He is fairly free from asthma, too. Had you noticed that? And he's stopped day-dreaming. Relief from eyestrain, this climate, work he loves — they're all good for him."

Between days of sailing, the Roosevelts made trips to see ancient temples, sometimes by day, often by moonlight. The beauty of desert scenes and old civilizations were inspiring when studied in this romantic way. The children acquired a feeling of time and history which few Americans of their day ever knew.

Back in Alexandria, Theodore got his new suit and shipped his trophies home. Then the family left for Jaffa and a journey through Palestine. In Jaffa the children were allowed to select their own horses while their father arranged camping equipment. Then they set off.

On the way Theodore and his father hunted and collected more birds. Theodore missed the comfort of the deck as a workshop but he did the best preserving he could. Each bird and animal was identified and a record put in his book. Often he worked late by the light of a primitive oil lamp.

This journey pleased them all, so when it ended they sailed for Beirut for another camping trip, this time to Damascus. On the way, Arab sheiks came to call, a sandstorm descended upon them, and they explored ancient caves and tunnels. But the most thrilling of all was the first view of Damascus, from a high cliff. Countless minarets, palaces, odd walls, made the place look the fairyland of Theodore's most fantastic stories.

About this time Mr. and Mrs. Roosevelt began to be concerned about schooling. Travel was fine; lessons occasional mornings were better than none. But the children would be spoiled if this luxurious life continued. In spite of protests from converts to a life of travel, horses were turned toward Beirut. The time had come for school and settled living.

Loyal Americans

The Roosevelts were crossing the desert, reluctant to end the journey, when Elliott, the healthy one, was suddenly ill. They hurried to the port city and sailed for Greece.

Theodore amused Corinne with stories and games. But the main part of each day he worked on the deck with new specimens. He had acquired skill in the taxidermy of birds, but his work now was with marine creatures which the sailors caught for him. Men watched as he skinned and prepared creatures large and small; treated the parts he wished to save, and then stuffed them into lifelike form.

"I don't see how Teedie can work with those men crowding so close," his mother worried one morning.

"Oh, he likes it, Mother," Anna laughed. "An audience always inspires him — you should know that."

Mr. Roosevelt found messages from New York at their landing place. A serious depression had fallen upon American business that spring of 1873, and by the end of the summer it became a frightening panic. Mr. Roosevelt, banker and merchant, sailed on the first ship for home.

Mrs. Roosevelt took the younger children to Germany, and put them in a well recommended home in Dresden, where they would have good care and tutoring. The cousins, John and Maude Elliott, and their mother, were living in Dresden, and the relatives planned to spend a day each week together. That done, Mrs. Roosevelt and Anna went to a quiet spa for a rest.

The five cousins were soon homesick. "I don't know which I hate more," Maude said on their first visit, "black bread or German verbs — the bread, I guess."

"The meat we have has no taste," Corinne complained. "It's boiled and boiled and boiled."

"I want pancakes for breakfast," John said, "and they don't understand what I mean."

"I like pancakes," Theodore admitted, "but if we were at home, we'd not be in the house of famous swordsmen. *That's* important!"

"Do they work at it?" Maude asked, paling.

"Not at home." Theodore grinned at her. "But you should

see them! The brother we call Sir Rhinoceros had the tip of his nose cut off in a duel. The other brother — we call him the Red Duke — has a long red scar on his face."

"I was frightened the first day he came home," Corinne admitted, "but I'm not any more. He is a kind man, very good to us. They are all good to us at our house."

"The Red Duke showed me their case of swords," Theodore went on. "I guess that is better than any old pancakes!"

"I wish he'd show me," John said. Pancakes were quickly forgotten.

The swordsmen's mother and sister took the Roosevelts on outings, and they did not fuss about snakes, frogs, and other creatures that Theodore brought home. His bureau drawers had to be opened cautiously; live creatures might pop out and dead ones smelled.

Lessons five days a week were in German language, literature, and other subjects. Theodore, who did not like English poetry, took a fancy to the ringing lines of the *Nibelungenlied*. He memorized long passages and recited them loudly in a voice that was apt to squeak unexpectedly. The children were taken to hear good German music, and Theodore liked that. Maude worried about his liking for German culture.

"I think we need something to remind us that we are Americans," she said as they were walking one day. "Even though we like living here we ought to be loyal Americans."

"*Loyal!*" Theodore stopped and stared at her, shocked. "We *are* loyal! Just say one word — "

"Oh, I know, Teedie," Maude soothed him quickly.

"Loyal!" Elliott sided with Maude. "No one would guess it to hear you spouting that German poetry."

"Well," Theodore studied this new viewpoint a moment, "we could organize an American society — just ourselves."

"It will have to be educational, or mother will say we are wasting our time." Corinne eyed her brother anxiously.

Theodore thought that over, too. "We could read American history or write about something — " his voice trailed off.

"What is there here to write about?" Elliott asked.

"Writing sounds like letters," Corinne said. "We do those. Of course if we could all draw pictures on edges like Teedie does for Father's — I make him let me see them."

"Well, we can't all draw," Maude said crisply. "Let's have a literary club and write original stories. That should sound important to parents."

The others liked her idea so the Dresden Literary American Club — D.L.A.C. for short — was organized. Meetings Sunday afternoons were to be with the cousins because they had no distracting German swordsmen at their house.

Members took their work seriously. At the first meeting Corinne brought two original poems and Theodore a long story which he entitled *Mrs. Field Mouse's Dinner Party.* The members listened critically as he read.

"I think it sounds like *Alice in Wonderland,*" Elliott commented frankly.

"It's fiction to illustrate social customs in America," the author informed him. "We're Americans — remember?"

"Read yours next, Maude," Corinne said quickly.

At the next meeting Theodore had an article on natural history which interested him more and the others less than his fiction. He used long Latin names, carefully spelled, for the animals mentioned; but English words of description were spelled to suit his fancy. Elliott had written a tragic tale called *The Bloody Hand,* and Corinne had more poems.

D.L.A.C. lasted for some weeks. Then Theodore had a terrifying return of asthma, and the Roosevelt children and their governess went to Switzerland. As soon as he recovered, he began writing a careful study comparing birds in Egypt and in Switzerland.

The return of Theodore's asthma was depressing. Even though he got better, the children began to talk of home. Letters and newspapers told that the panic had affected the whole country. It was no time for a banker to go back to Europe. Perhaps they had better come home, Mrs. Roosevelt wrote. They were very content to go.

The fifteen-year-old Theodore who returned to America was thin and spindly but healthier than a year before. An unruly lock of blond hair defied his efforts to keep it flat. Clothes sagged on narrow, drooping shoulders; skillful hands were always stained with chemicals; eager eyes peered through thick lenses and missed nothing. His chief concern on the voyage was for his precious trophies. In a high, uncertain voice he defended them against many hazards.

The Roosevelts settled in a new home at 6 West 57th Street. The children had not yet started school when Mr. Roosevelt announced that Theodore was to go to Harvard.

"Well, if you have decided," Mrs. Roosevelt said doubtfully. "He will need tutoring for entrance, I suppose. I hardly think he can go to school like the others."

"U-u-um, I doubt it," Mr. Roosevelt admitted reluctantly. "His education is uneven. He is good in science, history and geography — and of course French and German. But he is far behind in Latin, Greek, and Mathematics. I'll get a tutor."

An excellent young man was engaged and Elliott and Corinne had lessons with him, too, until they caught up on subjects they had missed. Then they went to school and the tutor and Theodore worked hard on college requirements.

To his astonishment, Theodore found that he did not know how to spell.

"People I wrote letters to never complained," he protested. "They knew what I meant. Why bother? Why need I make such an exact arrangement of letters?"

"If you work at Harvard, you will have to spell as Harvard spells," the tutor said, amused.

"Oh, well, then." Theodore conceded. He never did like spelling and too many letters in a word seemed silly. But he tackled spelling vigorously, as he did other subjects. Lessons, gymnasium, and boxing lessons filled his days.

That summer the Roosevelts moved to Oyster Bay, on Long Island, for the warm season. The location was a happy choice for Theodore; his health began to make steady improvement. He was on the water every day sailing and rowing. He enjoyed water sports; battling waves and wind thrilled him. He rode a great deal, too, and became a fairly good horseman, fearless on a hunt and good tempered with his tumbles.

In spite of his full program, which continued through the summer, Theodore managed to do some work in natural history. He enjoyed this so much that his father wondered if he meant to make that a life profession.

"The time is coming when you will have to choose your work, my son," he said. "If you are good at it, you can make a living as a scientist. But you cannot accumulate wealth."

"I wouldn't care, Father," Theodore said fervently. "I'd like to be an Audubon — Mr. Bell was his friend and told me about him. Maybe I would not be rich. But I'd enjoy it."

"Yes, and that is important to a man, maybe more important than things money can buy. My business prospers now, likely I can give you a modest sum each year to add to your earnings. But you would have to do without many pleasures — a stable of horses, boats, fine houses. If you care that much for science I hope you will continue with it. A man's work is life to him — remember that."

"I shall not forget. Do I need to decide now?"

"No, wait till after college. Then if you still care for science, strike out bravely and do what you want to do."

Theodore worked so successfully that he finished three years' work of preparation in two years. His father was proud and pleased.

During those same two years, the United States slowly struggled up from the depression. Factories in the East were hard at work; farmers in the West planted wheat and began to think about foreign trade. Money and honest government were topics for political arguments over the country.

But politics was not a usual topic of talk at the Roosevelt home on 57th Street; even less at Oyster Bay. Music, art, literature, and philanthropies were still the family interests. Mr. Roosevelt worked hard for a News Boys' Lodging House; the children were used to his spending Sunday evenings there. He helped raise money for an Orthopedic Hospital and was active in church work and in projects for the underprivileged. His was a busy, generous life, without politics. The young people never thought of the subject.

The Theodore Roosevelt, Jr., not quite eighteen, who set off for Harvard that autumn of 1876 looked very different from the earnest, tousled lad with the pipestem legs of other years. Blond hair was smooth; his fashionable suit was immaculate. He was thin, almost gaunt, five foot six in height, and of course wore those heavy spectacles. Students glanced at him without favor as they dashed about their own affairs. They did not guess that his air of hauteur was really a deep shyness surprising to Theodore himself. It was strange to be away from home.

Mr. Roosevelt had thought that dormitories might be damp and bring a return of asthma, so he had engaged rooms in a private house between the college and the Charles River. Theodore's sister Anna went up ahead to see that they were comfortable and well furnished.

"You will like this much better than a dormitory, Teedie," she told him as she left for home. "They promise me here that you can keep all your natural history specimens — you could never do that in a dormitory, you know."

"You've made the place so comfortable," Theodore gazed around with appreciation. "No one ever had such a wonderful family as mine!" Already he was coming down with the usual freshman malady — homesickness.

College Years

Cambridge, Massachusetts, by this year 1876, had seen changes since George Washington took command of the Continental Army on the village green one hundred and one years earlier.

Now plain red brick buildings surrounded Harvard Yard; daily living of villagers and the eight hundred students centered around Harvard Square nearby. From this square small horse-drawn street cars left hourly for Boston. In winter, the floor of these cars was bedded with straw, the only gesture toward comfort. In summer, the long ride was hot and stifling because car windows were nailed shut.

Freshman Roosevelt was clear about what he wanted from college. Perhaps because his education so far had been irregular, he now wanted the usual formal courses. He did not like President Eliot's new plan for elective courses; and he thought that students should be required to attend church. Partly as a protest, and of course to please his father, he decided to teach in Sunday School. There was no Dutch Reformed Church in Cambridge, but denominations seemed unimportant; he taught in an Episcopal Church.

In several ways he earned the reputation of being queer. He was very serious about his studies and often annoyed professors by asking endless questions. He liked to wander off, after classes, and search for natural history specimens, and he took up boxing though it was not one of the usual college sports. His only concession to current fashion was his new side whiskers — but even these looked odd because they grew out auburn, not blond to match his hair. All these small things combined to delay his making friends.

In October of that freshman year, Harvard students got up a huge torchlight parade to stir interest in the presidential campaign between Hayes and Tilden. Young men carried banners and transparencies — banners tacked around a wooden frame on a pole. On top of the pole, inside the frame, an oil lamp burned; this was very effective at night. Slogans on the banners were about currency, banking, tariff, and public lands — the campaign talk of many a season. Cambridge streets were crowded with shouting partisans.

In checking up later, an upperclassman asked where that young Roosevelt had marched. His father was a Republican.

"With freshman Republicans, I suppose," someone said.

"I doubt that," another replied, annoyed. "I didn't see him all evening. Likely he was in his room skinning snakes. He's not interested in parades." This verdict was unfortunate in a place where uniformity was important.

Theodore hardly noticed, or cared. He passed all his freshman courses with grades in the safe seventies and left with a friend, Harry Minot, for a tour of the Adirondack Mountains to study birds. Harry was a good companion. They observed and recorded accurately many birds. Later these notes were published as a catalogue entitled *The Summer Birds of the Adirondacks in Franklin County* by Theodore Roosevelt, Jr., and H. D. Minot. This was an unusual project for youths of their age.

After the bird study, Theodore went to Oyster Bay, where he enjoyed a wonderful summer. His health improved, and he was stronger and taller when he left for Cambridge in the fall.

"I shall dig in and study hard," he promised his father. "You will be pleased with my grades next June."

Because of this promise his mother did not tell him when his father was taken ill after the holidays. Hopefully she decided that there was no reason to worry her son in the midst of midyear examinations. So a message announcing his father's death was a terrible shock. Theodore stared at that yellow sheet — his father, so kind, so vigorous — he couldn't be *dead!*

"He was the best man I ever knew," Theodore exclaimed in a broken voice. "The best man I ever knew."

Suddenly he tossed the slip aside and rushed to Boston and a train for New York. As it clicked over the rails, he began to feel a heavy burden upon him. He was the older son; he was now the head of the family. The thought of all his father had done for him appalled him. His father would expect him to be brave now, and to help his family.

This duty to others sustained him through the difficult days that followed in New York and continued when he returned to college. He studied hard and brought up his grades; he got a 96 in German, 94 in rhetoric; and all grades were well above those of freshman year.

As he planned his junior courses he suddenly realized that he no longer dreamed of being a great scientist.

"I could never prepare as I should," he remarked to a classmate, "not the way natural science is taught here."

"Harvard is advanced in science — what's wrong, Thee?"

"Oh, professors are interested only in minutiae; in microscopic slides, cells, laboratory work . . ."

"What do you want, man! Scientists have to learn!"

"Yes," Theodore granted. "But I want to be an outdoor naturalist. Laboratory study is fine for those who want it. I prefer study in the woods where animals belong." His face was alight with eagerness.

"You'll be unpopular with the professors. They study down to the last cell."

"Thoroughness is fine. That's not my objection . . ."

"Maybe your eyes . . ."

"No. I see well with glasses," Theodore retorted quickly. He resented any hint of disability. "I'm just bored. I like animals in the open and professors have another point of view."

For a while Theodore thought of being a writer. A high mark on an English theme encouraged him. He considered law. It was hard to plan; he had been sure science would be his profession. Possibly the distaste he now felt came from the years when he could see only what lay close at hand. Since he first saw the beautiful world that day he put on glasses, the outdoors had fascinated him. He could not tear it to bits, not even for study.

He finally decided to take one natural history course each year and to broaden his study in other subjects, especially preparation for writing. He did not study public speaking, and he declined an invitation to join a debating society.

"Come around and visit us," the classmate who suggested his name said. "We learn to argue all sides and to talk on our feet. You may change your mind."

Theodore went, and was astonished at the vigor of the arguments. On the way home he took his friend to task.

"I had no idea you believed as you talked in that debate," he said frankly. The classmate chuckled.

"I don't. We don't have to believe what we say in speeches. This is a debate, and we have to be broad-minded and take whichever side we are assigned."

"I'd never do that!" Young Roosevelt flushed hotly. "I'd not argue against my conviction." Theodore's tone was stern.

"That's narrow-minded and stuffy. I'm surprised at you!"

"It's not narrow; it's honest. I agree a man should study all sides of a question *before* he makes up his mind. But once I'd decided, I'd argue only for what I thought right."

"And you talk of being a lawyer! Lawyers have to take whichever side hires them . . ."

"Not me," Theodore interrupted. "I shall never take a case until I know it is right."

"You'll make a very poor living then," scoffed his friend. But Theodore was not persuaded to join that society.

The early part of Theodore's junior year was marked by two important events. The first was a serious effort at writing.

He liked American history and had read a good deal of it, especially during the previous summer. He had not found a clear, honest history of the Naval War of 1812 so he resolved to dig out the facts and write about it himself. This would be more interesting, he thought, than subjects the professors handed out.

The second event occurred a little before his twentieth birthday in October; he met a beautiful girl and immediately was deeply in love.

Alice Lee was not his first feminine interest; he had known several girls, some of Corinne's friends. Of these, he especially liked Edith Carow, a close friend of Corinne since childhood. Theodore had written to Edith on his European travels; Edith and Corinne had come to Cambridge for parties. He had always admired her.

But tall, willowy, curly-haired Alice Lee was different. He found her entrancing and resolved to marry her at the first possible moment. Sundays, Theodore rushed from Sunday School and drove to Chestnut Hill where Alice lived.

Spring and fall, he took Alice driving and to parties in a fashionable "dog-cart." In winter, when snow lay on the ground, he drove a sleigh. With bells jingling and bright scarves flying they felt very gay and happy. Those were thrilling weekends.

The rest of the time he toiled at languages, logic, and other profound subjects, and somehow managed to read a good deal of naval history. He had little time for writing, because he faithfully kept on trying to make himself strong by walking, boxing, and skipping rope.

Young Roosevelt's enthusiasm for boxing was the cause

of many a tale circulated around the campus. A favorite told of a match between Theodore and an outsider of much vaunted size and prowess. Quite a crowd had gathered to see the smaller man brought to defeat.

As the story was told, the two were facing each other when Roosevelt glanced down to adjust the fastening of his glove. Instantly, his opponent struck Roosevelt a hard blow to the jaw.

"Foul! Foul!" the crowd yelled angrily.

"Throw him out!"

Theodore's face was scarlet where the blow hit; a dribble of blood streaked downward; his lips were a stern line. But he did not look up until the glove was adjusted.

Then he spoke, politely. "I guess you did not know our

rules. Here, we salute before we fight." He extended his right hand in a formal salute. The opponent stared, astonished.

The two gloved hands had barely touched when Theodore's fist shot out with terrific force. In two minutes the visiting boxer was down and out. After that, Theodore was known to all the students!

Gradually he made a place for himself at Harvard. In the spring of his senior year, his engagement to Alice Lee was announced, and they planned their wedding for October. He wrote two chapters of his naval history; got honorable mention in natural science and was elected to the honor society, Phi Beta Kappa. All this meant that he worked hard and liked it.

The Theodore Roosevelt who marched with his class of one hundred and seventy young men was much changed from the shy youth who had entered college. He still skipped rope for exercise but the red whiskers were gone and in all important matters he was earnest and successful — and he had friends.

After commencement, Theodore and Elliott went on a long hunting trip. Strangely enough, as Theodore grew out of invalidism, Elliott, who had been a strong lad, had bad health. Perhaps he never quite recovered from that desert fever he had after they were in Damascus. Elliott did not go to college; instead he spent months in the west and southwest. He was an excellent shot and enjoyed hunting.

The brothers had a wonderful time on this trip. Their letters told of hunting and tramping through Iowa and Minnesota. For a New Yorker, that was the West. They proudly boasted of heavy beards and good shooting.

But promptly on their return, Theodore shaved off that beard and took the train for Chestnut Hill and Alice. He could hardly wait to see her.

They were married on Theodore's twenty-second birthday — Alice was nineteen — and they went to live with his widowed mother in the spacious home on West 57th Street. They intended to take a wedding trip abroad but the journey was postponed for the present because Theodore had decided to be a lawyer. He was enrolled at Columbia University Law School and was eager to begin his studies. He hoped his choice of profession was wise — it was hard to be sure when so many kinds of work were interesting.

Theodore Discovers Politics

In a short time, Roosevelt saw that his doubts about law as the profession for him were natural. The law books were very boring. But he could not bring himself to give it up without a fair trial.

As he faithfully kept at work, he made a thrilling discovery: the human side of law was fascinating. Impatiently, he searched books and talked with men, trying to find out why laws were as they were and how well laws served the people. Was justice done rich and poor? How was the city governed? Did the people in his own neighborhood take part in government? Questions that had never occurred to him before now seemed important.

The Roosevelts entertained a good deal, and Theodore often talked with his friends about his new interest. From them, and from law school, he learned about ward politics and city government — new and lively topics to him now.

"I'm going to visit the Republican Club of our ward tomorrow evening," he remarked to a guest at dinner.

"Really? Why bother?" the man asked in surprise. "A political club is no place for a gentleman. You'll meet saloon keepers, horse-car conductors, stablemen — just common folk."

"These men run *our* ward?" Theodore asked.

"Of course. Don't mix with them."

"But sir, if these 'common folk' run our ward, then they are the ruling class. I want to know them." The guest stared.

"That's an odd point of view," he said and turned away.

The Twenty-first District Republican Association in the City of New York met twice a month in Morton Hall, a huge, poorly furnished room over a saloon. Other nights, the place was used as a social club, open to members of the association. Roosevelt went to the first meeting after he got this information.

As he entered the big room, men eyed him uneasily. His clothes were different from theirs; his thick glasses were a novelty. Their clothes and manners seemed equally odd to him, and he had no idea that he was invading a club where membership was by invitation. He looked around, getting his bearings, as the ward "boss" came over toward him.

"Jake Hess is the name," the man said coolly. "And yours?"

"Theodore Roosevelt, sir. May I attend your meeting?"

Hess was not cordial, but Roosevelt stayed. Soon one of the lesser officers spoke to him in a more friendly way.

"Good evening, sir. Joe Murray is the name. This is the Twenty-first District Republican Association — "

"Yes, that's why I came," Roosevelt said. "I'd like to join." Joe shook hands, but he did not mention membership. Soon the meeting began.

"I like Joe Murray," Roosevelt said to his wife when he told her about the meeting. "I think he likes me."

"What does he do?" Alice asked. She was not much interested in Joe Murray, but her husband fascinated her. She liked to hear him talk when he was happy, as now.

"Joe is Irish. I asked around about him. He and his parents landed in New York when Joe was a toddler — he calls himself 'the barefoot boy of First Avenue.' He is fearless and strong; served in the Civil War. He's a leader of a gang and honest as they come. I hope we shall be friends."

Roosevelt attended all the regular meetings after that, and sometimes dropped in on other evenings. The talk he heard there interested him more than law books. Some weeks later, Joe Murray told him that he had been accepted as a member.

"This is really an honor," Theodore told Alice, later. "I'm the only member from our neighborhood. I am proud that they have accepted me." He paused thoughtfully, and then added, "I have a hunch that Joe has some plan in his head. He says that voters are angry and upset since the last election."

"Did he tell you why?"

"Not exactly," Theodore told her. "I know a Tammany man was elected. I hear that he made a lot of promises to voters before the election and then did not keep his word.

"I heard Joe say that there might be a chance for a Republican to be elected to the legislature. If that comes true, I'd like to help Joe — but I wouldn't know what to do. Joe is all worked up about it. He is not afraid of Tammany."

"What's Tammany?" Alice asked.

"It's a powerful organization of Democrats; it controls New York City. I've heard of it — I ought to look it up."

Digging into history the next day, Roosevelt was surprised to find that Tammany had a patriotic beginning after the Revolutionary War. Then veteran officers started a society to help each other when in trouble. Soon veteran privates got up their own society and named it Tammany. In those days before life insurance and pensions, such organizations were important. By 1820 Tammany was working to abolish imprisonment for debt, and for more liberal suffrage — both were needed reforms.

As years passed, Tammany grew, and became more powerful in politics. The leader was called the "Boss" and took to himself great authority. As often happens, corruption crept in along with power.

Ten years before Roosevelt first visited Morton Hall, Boss Tweed had got Tammany men elected to city jobs. Citizens allowed these men to steal city taxes and to increase the city's debt by millions. Taxes allotted for street cleaning went into Tammany pockets. Filthy streets and alleys were an evil symbol of Tammany's power and of public indifference.

"Can't we clean up our streets?" Roosevelt boldly inquired at a meeting soon after he became a member.

Men stared, astonished. And then they roared with laughter. The man next to him tried to explain.

"You'd have to get a lot of backing —"

"Backing?" Roosevelt asked.

"People to help you make a fight. You can't win against Tammany."

"We can try." He made a campaign of it and created quite a stir. They didn't win. But the effort had been thrilling.

Undiscouraged, he attended meetings until spring. Then he and Alice sailed for their wedding journey in Europe.

"I've packed my notes on naval history, Mother," Theodore said as they drove to the wharf. "While we're traveling I shall

finish my book. Remember how we children always worked mornings when we were traveling? I shall do the same."

His mother smiled, affectionately. She was glad he had such a memory, but she wondered how much writing he would do.

The Roosevelts saw sights in a happy, leisurely way. The book was a nagging worry — when Theodore thought of it, which was seldom.

But late in the summer, while Theodore and Alice were visiting in England, the uncles aroused his interest.

"You mean to tell me you've not finished it?" Uncle Jimmy scolded. "Bring it down. I'll see what you've written."

"Oh, it's not half done," Theodore was chagrined. "To tell you the truth, Uncle, I've got notes on the history. But the kinds of ships and all that are beyond me."

"You have certainly come to the right place, Nephew," Uncle Irvine announced. "Get your papers. Likely Jimmy and I can tell you what you want to know."

Their enthusiasm and their nautical knowledge were exactly what Theodore needed. He worked hard and finished the manuscript. It was published the next year, 1882 — his first book.

When the Roosevelts were back in New York, Theodore found that his hunch about Joe Murray had been correct. Joe did have a plan. Moreover it concerned the new member.

"You're to run for the state legislature from this district," Joe told Roosevelt. Theodore was astonished.

"I could never be elected," Roosevelt exclaimed. "I don't know politics. I'd not even get the nomination!"

"You leave that to me. All you need do is accept."

Roosevelt talked the idea over at home. His mother feared it would interrupt his studies.

"You are right, Mother. It would. But it is an opportunity. I think I will not be elected; but if I am, I would have a chance to learn more than books can teach and I might do some good — I would certainly try. I shall accept."

Joe was right; Roosevelt was nominated. Election, of course, would be much harder to win. But Joe had that planned, too, and began introducing his candidate.

One night Jake and Joe, with some misgivings, took the candidate around to meet some Sixth Avenue voters. Naturally they began at a saloon. Roosevelt was introduced to the owner, an important man in the business, who proceeded to cross-question the young man. His manner showed that he did not think well of being represented by a twenty-three-year-old.

"I hope you will treat saloons fairly," he began.

"I expect to be fair in all my dealings," Roosevelt retorted, annoyed at the implication.

"You know that licenses are too high — "

"On the contrary," Roosevelt interrupted. "I consider that licenses are not high enough. I shall do my best, if elected, to have them raised." The saloon keeper flushed.

"Sorry, but we have a lot of calls to make — " Joe Murray hurried to the rescue and eased his candidate out of that place fast.

"I'll tell you, Mr. Roosevelt," Murray said when they were outside. "I think we must divide up this campaign work. You take care of your friends of Fifth Avenue and I'll deliver the votes on Sixth." It proved to be a good division of labor, for Roosevelt was elected assemblyman from the Twenty-first District. His margin of votes was comfortable: 3400 to 1989.

Roosevelt was pleased that the New York *Times* praised him as a public-spirited citizen; and support from his father's friends was gratifying. But he knew that, actually, Joe Murray and Jake Hess had won that election. He resolved that he would not forget them, as they feared he might. Neither did he intend to favor them.

December, 1881, drew to a close and the Theodore Roosevelts went to Albany for the opening of the State Assembly on January second. They settled in rooms in a small hotel and prepared to devote themselves to the new work. Albany was a crude town compared with New York; they would find few social pleasures such as they were used to enjoying. So, since the legislature closed Friday afternoons, they planned to spend week ends with Mrs. Roosevelt, senior, in New York.

Roosevelt was the youngest member of the Assembly. Now at twenty-three, he had attained his full growth, five feet ten inches, and his health was good. Occasional attacks of asthma were annoying, but not serious.

On the day the Assembly opened in the big unfinished Capitol, he felt uplifted, dedicated, eager to serve his state. Probably he thought often of his father; the older man would have been proud of his son's vigor and this opportunity for public service. Men who chanced to notice the new member, the day the Assembly opened, observed an earnest, serious, young man who wore heavy glasses dangling fashionably from a black ribbon.

A prompt appointment to the City Affairs Committee was logical since Roosevelt came from New York, but he had no program and no idea how to make himself effective. His natural curiosity kept him active, and twice he attempted to speak. Words eluded him and then rushed forth so fast men could hardly understand. The whole experience was puzzling to him.

"Laws governing primaries need reform," he told his wife. "And I should do something about Civil Service. Father thought it so wrong to change all government employees with each change of administration."

"How do other Republican members stand?" Mrs. Roosevelt enjoyed talking with him.

"That doesn't matter," he waved the idea aside. "I shall stand for what I think is right, regardless. Anyway, Alice, party lines make little difference here. The Assembly is Democratic, yes. But they are split, Tammany and anti-Tammany. This might give an independent Republican a good chance."

Roosevelt made friends quickly. Six years, and his experiences at Morton Hall had changed the shy young man who had entered Harvard. Now men of all sorts interested him. Young Billy O'Neil, keeper of a crossroads store in the Adirondacks, became his favorite companion. With Billy he gathered a circle of independent thinkers who talked for hours about Abraham Lincoln and his ideas of government. In the group was a New York reporter who was helpful in digging into affairs of the Elevated Railway. Roosevelt did not yet have legal proof, but he felt sure that some of their dishonest acts were connected with the state's attorney and a state supreme court judge.

In April, Roosevelt rose confidently in the Assembly and boldly demanded the impeachment of that judge.

Members stared in shocked silence. How dared a man risk his whole future with such bold action? Roosevelt was too young; that was his trouble. He did not know what he was doing! Hardly a member doubted his charges; but truth should not be so recklessly displayed in public. The Republican leaders hastily decided to treat the speech as the ignorant act of a callow youth, not worthy of notice.

They did not know Theodore Roosevelt. As though inspired, Roosevelt gave interviews and was quoted in newspapers in New York City and throughout the state. The public was aroused; letters poured in on assemblymen and the governor. They were compelled to notice the charges. By an overwhelming vote, an investigation was ordered.

Telling of Roosevelt's speech later, an assemblyman said, "He stood there like a David, hurling pebbles at a giant. His words spilled out — blurred at times with his excitement. But we knew he meant what he said. I was sure he was wrecking his career before he'd started."

"It was one of the bravest acts I ever saw," another said.

When the Assembly closed a few weeks later Roosevelt was a marked man — never again could he be obscure or unknown.

Back in New York, he was restless. Law studies never did absorb his interest. His naval history was published and reviews were excellent. It was praised in his own country and in England. Soon he was asked to write a chapter on the War of 1812 for the official history of the British Royal Navy.

He bought a partnership in a publishing house, and thought of writing another book. In August he joined the National Guard and was faithful and interested in military drilling. None of this brought income, and the legislature paid only $1,500 a year. To be sure he had an income from his share in his father's estate, but that, as his father had told him, was for "bread." With an attractive young wife, he wanted "butter and jam" too. His new difficulty was that he could not figure out how to get luxuries *and* serve society; such work had begun to intrigue him.

That fall he was re-elected to the state legislature by an increased majority, and he plunged deeper into politics. The opportunity that Joe Murray had given him and that he had had the courage to grasp, opened a new world to young Theodore Roosevelt.

"The Cyclone Hero"

His re-election gave Theodore Roosevelt a glow of pride. He felt sure now, he had found the career he wanted. New York papers had written of his "daring" and "faithfulness"; he determined to work even harder for the people he represented. When the assembly convened he was made the minority leader, the youngest man to hold that post.

Promptly a bill to lower fares on the elevated railway in New York City came up. A similar bill defeated the year before had had an odor of corruption about it. Roosevelt did not analyze this new bill; lower fares seemed a fine idea for the people. O'Neil and others he knew joined him in work for it and the bill was passed. Then Governor Cleveland vetoed it! Roosevelt was amazed. What was wrong?

"This bill is unconstitutional," Cleveland said as he returned it. "The legislature cannot regulate fares."

Roosevelt now studied the bill and saw Cleveland was right. Some tried to pass it over the veto. Roosevelt stopped that by an unheard-of move; he announced himself mistaken.

"I say with shame that when I voted for this bill I did not act as I ought to have acted," he said boldly. "Legislators must support existing laws. I would rather go out of politics feeling I had done right than stay, knowing I had acted as I ought not to have done." The veto was sustained.

Some New York newspapers jeered; one called it "Roosevelt's dying speech."

Those that approved spoke of his characteristic manliness. Both friends and foes said he was ruined politically.

Undaunted, Roosevelt worked for several controversial bills. One concerned freedom of the press; another, state funds for church institutions; another, civil service for New York City employees. Even when bills failed to pass, the subjects were brought up for public attention. That was good.

After all this strenuous work, Roosevelt yearned for a vacation in the open. He had chanced to hear of good buffalo hunting in the Bad Lands of Dakota Territory and decided that would be the perfect diversion. The new Northern Pacific Railroad took him to the town called Little Missouri, a small group of buildings which were no more than shacks, on the river by the same name.

His search for a guide and equipment led him to the Ferris brothers, Joe and Sylvane, and Sylvane's partner, Merrifield. Thanks to these men, Roosevelt had his hunt and got a handsome buffalo head for a trophy. More important, he became intrigued with ranching and the delights of the West.

"This is going to be great cattle country," they told him. "Buffalo no longer roam in herds — "

"Indians have gone, too," another said. "Dakota is safe; it ought to be a state soon. Land will boom. The man in early will make a killing."

The tenderfoot from the big city wanted to believe. The dry, clear air invigorated him. The winding river, the picturesque buttes — irregular hills rising from parched land — were interesting; he did not notice the sparse, brown grass. Before he went back East he bought the Maltese Cross Ranch near Chimney Butte, a conspicuous landmark some eight miles down the river. Later he bought a second ranch, the Elkhorn, further down the stream. This latter place was ideal for a ranch residence. A grove of cottonwoods was nearby, and higher lands across the river made a beautiful view.

"You understand I cannot stay out here," he told men who congratulated him on a wise buy. "I hope to get Bill Sewall and his nephew, Will Dow, both Maine woodsmen I can trust, to come out here and run the places for me."

"But you'll come out sometimes?"

"I wouldn't miss the fun!" Roosevelt grinned contentedly.

"I'll come once a year at least!" Then he took the train for New York and his third campaign for legislature.

Republicans won control of the House, and Roosevelt polled his biggest majority. Naturally he hoped to be the Speaker, but another man was elected. He became chairman of the Cities Committee and a special committee to propose reforms in New York City. He took these assignments seriously, arranged visits of inspection with his committee, and worked hard.

This year his young wife did not go to Albany. They were expecting the birth of a child in February, so she stayed in New York and he went down for weekends. His sister Corinne, now Mrs. Douglas Robinson, and her husband and baby son were in the 57th Street home that winter, so Alice was not lonely.

The expected telegram was handed to Roosevelt on the morning of the thirteenth. His daughter was born and his wife was doing well. He left at once for home.

Glowing with happiness he dashed up his front steps. Elliott opened the door. A glance at his face showed Theodore that something was wrong.

"Mother and Alice are dying," Elliott blurted out. "If you want to see either of them alive — hurry!"

Theodore staggered up the stairs and into his wife's room. She barely recognized him. In the night he was called to his mother's bedside as she died of typhoid fever that had been thought only a minor illness. From that deathbed he returned to his wife and held her in his arms until she died. The shocked stillness of the stricken household was broken only by the plaintive cry of the newborn baby.

On the day of the service, crowds gathered. People bowed in silence as two hearses, side by side, slowly moved to the church. Two coffins were carried forward to the flower-decked chancel; two graves were finally closed.

Some time later, Theodore Roosevelt wrote a memorial to Alice Lee Roosevelt. In moving, poetic words he told of her beauty and sweet character. Then he seemed to close her tightly in his heart; he rarely, if ever, spoke of her again.

Life and work must go on. Corinne promised to care for the baby, named Alice for her lovely mother. In a few days Roosevelt went to Albany to continue his work.

The reform bills were in trouble. The City Committee had plenty of evidence to prove the need for new laws but "interests" were skillful in delaying action.

"The public must know facts," Roosevelt told the committee. Many newspapers were glad to print what he sent.

The final days when the bills were up for voting were exciting. Reporters flocked to Albany — even city newspapers broke with custom and sent correspondents. Reports came out under stirring headlines such as

"THEODORE, THE CYCLONE HERO OF THE ASSEMBLY"

Cartoons, by now important in political affairs, covered full pages. One showed Roosevelt brandishing huge scissors and about to cut the Tammany Tiger's sharp claws.

Some of the bills to improve methods of governing the city passed. Two that Roosevelt most cherished failed. But newspapers still praised his efforts toward public good.

"Roosevelt has shown boldness and energy," one said.

"He inspired his associates with his zeal for reform."

The session had one more important bill, the one promoted by the Cigar Makers' Union to end making cigars in tenement homes. Many legislators were puzzled about this bill. Roosevelt went to New York several times, alone and with his committee, to learn facts he ought to know.

At that time cigars were made by the poorest of New York's poor, the newly arrived immigrants. These people spoke no English and could not compete for work. Whole families toiled long hours for wages that would not buy a decent living.

Roosevelt led the committee up rickety stairs, down into damp basements. He showed them rooms where two families lived — and made cigars — in one dark room, noisome, filthy; even the children had gaunt faces.

"Do you gentlemen want to smoke cigars made in there?" he asked them when they were back on the street. He did not use tobacco; they did, and they were dismayed.

"Law must take manufacture out of such places," they said. New efforts were put forth to make a better law.

This attempt in the early 1880's to have a product made under healthy conditions was very bold. Many said that Roosevelt's concern showed he was a youthful Don Quixote rather than a sensible legislator. Apparently no one on the committee thought that something might be done for the people as well as for the cigars. The social conscience was sleeping soundly in those years.

The bill passed. Later the courts ruled that the bill was unconstitutional — why? Because a man had the right to do what he pleased in his home! Roosevelt raged in vain.

That spring of 1884 New York State elected four delegates-at-large for the National Republican Convention held at Chicago in June. Roosevelt was one of the four. He was beginning to be known around the country as a hard-working, excitable young man who was too idealistic to get far. But he was always noticed; they sent him to the Convention even though he did not favor the popular candidate for president, James G. Blaine. Roosevelt had come out for Edmunds, a quiet Vermonter.

After the usual fanfare and oratory Blaine was nominated. Roosevelt stormed out of the hall in a rage.

"That man for our president?" he cried furiously.

"Republicans nominated him," some bystanders remarked.

"Blaine's not wanted by Republicans over the country," Roosevelt retorted. Reporters gathered.

"Will you bolt the party, Mr. Roosevelt?" they asked.

The question alerted Roosevelt and he calmed down.

"You know my stand. I have nothing to add at this time."

Through his anger, he saw that he must think the matter over before he talked for publication. He got his bags and took the train for Dakota.

Thoughts raced through Roosevelt's mind as the engine streaked west. Just where did he stand in life? He had learned to work with men, a difficult lesson for one whose boyhood had been isolated from groups. He had learned to stand on his feet and control the torrent of words so that listeners could get his ideas. He was fearless when his convictions were challenged.

But defeat of his candidate at the convention discouraged him. Had personal grief weakened his power to fight? He was almost crushed by a deep sense of failure.

"Shall I ever again take part in public life?" he asked himself. The answer was a clear and definite, "No."

The Dashing Cowboy

Joe Ferris met the train and waited around while Roosevelt bought some cowboy clothes at the small general store. Then they drove to Elkhorn Ranch.

The new owner approved the two-room cabin, built during the winter; he liked the study where he expected to write between hours of ranching. Then he lugged his duffle bag to his room; he could hardly wait to take off city clothes and get into that cowboy outfit he had just bought.

The fringed buckskin shirt, the horsehide *chaparajos,* the cowboy boots, gave him a deep feeling of satisfaction. Each article fitted perfectly. He put on the wide sombrero and peered hopefully into the tiny shaving mirror. He could see very little, but he was certain he looked the dashing cowboy he felt.

Next he selected a braided bridle and silver spurs from his bag and turned to pick up a weapon — which should it be? He had brought several with him; a heavy Sharps rifle, a double-barrelled English Express, a Winchester Rifle and a Colt revolver. He chose the revolver and stalked outdoors.

"Got a mount ready for me, Joe?"

"Sure have, Boss. Coming right up!"

Roosevelt waited by the corral gate, liking the feel of the buckskin shirt and the revolver. A glance down at the fringe suddenly brought a vivid memory of adored heroes of boyhood reading — Daniel Boone and Davy Crockett. He need not be ashamed, now, as he thought of them. No longer was he a sickly lad, propped on pillows to breathe. He was a man, taking his place in a man's land.

Joe brought a dancing pony, and Roosevelt mounted. With a splatter of gravel, he whirled and galloped away. When he felt safely remote from the ranch house, he fired his revolver several times, recklessly, pointing to the sky. Then he lay forward over the pony as they dashed over rough ground.

"D'you hear that?" a cowhand exclaimed, staring after the distant rider. "The boss sure feels good — or something. What's got into him?"

"I reckon he just feels like he acts, sort of free," Joe remarked. "He's a city fellow; kind of a dude, I reckon. He fancies himself in those clothes."

"Acts like a kid," the cowboy said, puzzled. "How old d'you say he was, Joe?"

"I didn't say," Joe answered with an edge to his voice. "I reckon he's twenty-five. He's the boss — remember?"

For two hours Roosevelt galloped; his mind was blown free of sorrow, care, problems. He felt like a boy — but not the boy *he* had been. That puny lad had never played cops and robbers;

had never dressed up for fun with other boys. In this new open country Roosevelt seemed refreshed, renewed. When he turned back toward the ranch house he was ready for hard work.

The cowboys were polite and very formal with him. They could see that the new boss was friendly, but he surely was queer. He did not smoke or swear, they had heard, and his thick spectacles and the nickname "Four-eyes" would be hard to live down. His priggish talk was an added barrier; often he used words they had never heard and they had to guess his meaning. And of course he did not understand their slang; in time he learned, but he never used such talk himself.

This part of America he had chosen was a portion of the great belt of land that stretched from the Rio Grande to British America. His ranches lay in the Upper Missouri basin, a rolling, broken plain. Rainfall was light. Streams, often nearly dry, swelled into raging torrents after a storm or were hidden by masses of ice in winter. Trees were scarce except for cottonwoods near rivers and a few cedars. In places volcanic action and erosion had made strange hills, called buttes, like Chimney Butte on his own land. The area along the Little Missouri River was called the Bad Lands because it was desolate and hard going for travelers.

Indians and noble hunters of the Boone type were gone. Even the greedy but courageous fur hunters who followed were gone, too. Buffalo and small creatures had been killed for their profitable fur. Cattlemen were taking the place of hunters. Skilled ranchers came up from the South. Unskilled men like Roosevelt came from the East and bought herds of long-horned cattle to feed on the wide unfenced plains.

Though his mind was absorbed in all this, Roosevelt was nagged by a fear that he was failing his party. He liked the idea of thinking independently; but he believed in a two-party system of government. He disapproved of Blaine; but Blaine was the Republican nominee for president. It was a puzzle.

In July Roosevelt went East for a conference, and agreed to help with campaigning in the fall. He brought Bill Sewall and Will Dow back with him, and the newcomers went to work at the building. Cottonwoods from a grove at a distance would supply the wood. Roosevelt liked to chop wood, so he helped; a tree fell here, another there; he wandered out of sight.

"How many have you-all chopped today?" he heard a cowboy ask, beyond the brush.

"Well," Bill Sewall paused. Roosevelt could fancy he put his foot on a stump to think. "Will chopped forty-nine. I did fifty-one, and the boss beavered down seventeen."

Roosevelt glanced at the trunk he was chopping and chuckled. His ax marks did look like a beaver's tooth-prints.

The most exciting part of a ranchman's work was the spring and fall round-up. Roosevelt planned his campaign trip so he could share that experience. Each ranch, or group of ranches, sent a team to spread out, circle-wise, and draw inward, bringing in all stray cattle. Roosevelt's group had a large region along the Little Missouri and they sent cowboys to join other roundups where their cattle might have strayed. All were to meet at an appointed place where each calf would be branded with the brand of the cow it followed.

Cowboys worked in teams and each had his own string of ponies to use in relays as the riding was long and hard. Roosevelt liked the names cowboys gave their ponies; Water Skip, Fall Back, Wirefence, Hackaback. His own favorite was Manitou, an almost perfect mount. Manitou would come when called, stand while being saddled, and go like the wind. He liked bread and often pushed his head in at the ranch house door, coaxing for a piece.

The cowboys were hardy, self-reliant men who understood cattle and were not lawless as Easterners fancied. Most were from the Southwest and in their talk and manners there was a suggestion of Spanish. Roosevelt soon adopted the shirt and knotted tie; he tucked his trousers into high-heeled boots and kept his revolver handy for rattlesnakes, and for small game which helped out a tiresome diet. He hung a lasso from his saddle horn, but he doubted whether he could ever learn cowboy skill in using it.

Riding some miles from the roundup location, Roosevelt and his cowboy teammate noticed smoke.

"What do we do about that?" he asked, pointing. "The herds will starve if the grass burns off."

The cowboy shrugged, indifferent — until they rounded a curious butte and saw a sheet of flame ahead.

"Yi-ho!" he yelled and, grabbing his lasso, flung it expertly over the nearest steer. Like a flash, he was off his pony and had slashed the steer into two gory halves.

"Rope'r here!" he yelled at his boss as he tightened his lasso around one-half the carcass, bloody side down. Roosevelt

quickly did the same with the other half.

"Come along!" the cowboy shouted and in minutes from their first glimpse of the flames, they were making an effective fire lane with those reeking carcasses. Flames were checked; grass was saved.

The whole round-up was a thrilling experience; Roosevelt was glad he had shared it.

He did his campaigning in the East, and later went home for a brief Christmas stay with his sister. Then he returned to the ranch and settled down for a comfortable routine of ranch work and writing. He was doing a series of articles on the West for *Century Magazine*. Frederick Remington illustrated them and the articles proved so successful that they were published as a book, *Hunting Trips of a Ranchman.*

Roosevelt's love of beauty surprised readers who had known him only as a politician. People came to know the long, low ranch house those Maine woodsmen had built; to think of the plaintive autumn cry of the migrating water fowl, the weird howl of the coyote at night, or the chirp of snow buntings. His pen ranged from the pack-rat to the grizzly — but he liked birds the best.

Along with writing, Roosevelt gave a thought to the tiresome diet at the ranch. He missed milk and butter most. So he contrived to find a few more or less tame cows in the herd and to keep them in a fenced section. He raised chickens and finally killed off enough bobcats and coyotes to make the poultry relatively safe.

The job of getting fresh meat was soon added to his other duties. On Manitou, he hunted far and brought home ducks, antelope, and sometimes bigger game. Often he was gone for several days. Fur gloves and a coonskin coat kept him warm in winter, and at night he slept in a buffalo-hide sleeping bag.

Roosevelt liked all the experiences of ranch life. But he soon learned that there was little in it of the stirring drama that Easterners imagined. Day after day was filled with hard work, hard riding, and endless chores. His most exciting experience of those years came unexpectedly; not with wild animals, but with boat thieves.

At Elkhorn Ranch the river flowed through grazing land and some of the best grass was on the far side. In summer the river was a series of quiet pools that a flash flood turned into a powerful, deep stream. Crossing to check the herds was quite a chore.

The men from Maine built a boat, the best on the river, and crossing became easy. In winter ranchmen dragged the boat over ice to open water and then launched it. Because of that boat Roosevelt could keep larger herds.

On a March morning in '86, cowboys went to cross the river as usual. They ran back shouting, "The boat's gone!"

"Those horse thieves!" Merrifield cried angrily.

"Why would *horse* thieves want a *boat?*" Roosevelt asked.

"To get out of the neighborhood," two or three answered.

"Maybe we didn't tell you," Bill remarked. "Will heard yesterday that the stolen horses were caught, but the men got away before they were shot."

"In our boat they can easily escape," Will said thoughtfully. "We can't follow them on horses — no road's near the river. And no one else has a boat we could borrow. Smart, those boys are!"

Roosevelt's eyes blazed. "Who built that only boat?"

"Me 'n Bill," Will grinned. "I see we're elected to build another one. But it took us a while, Mr. Roosevelt."

"Build the best you can, boys; speed is essential."

In three days a raftlike boat was ready, and loaded with blankets and food for two weeks. With their guns and plenty of ammunition Roosevelt and the men from Maine boarded and pushed off. Those left on shore were quiet; this was no picnic.

To Roosevelt the expedition was more important than getting back stolen property. He cared more for justice and law than for that boat. In a wild country, like this, no policemen, no courts, protected people. A man who was robbed had to catch the thieves himself. If he let them go, the land would soon be overrun with robbers — decent settlers would not come. Those men must be caught.

A blizzard had been blowing, but the sun came out as they left. The wind died. Swift currents whirled them down the stream narrowed by ice. At night they camped on a sandy point; prairie fowl they shot made a supper. They curled under blankets; keeping on heavy coats, gloves, and boots.

The next day was colder, down to zero. Ice froze on the poles; water was icy slush; the going hard. They shot a deer the next morning and agreed there must be no more shooting and only whispered talk. The thieves might be near.

"Hist! There they are!" Roosevelt whispered tensely, as they rounded a bend in the late afternoon. The stolen boat was tied to the bank on ahead; smoke rose from a thicket.

In careful silence Bill turned their craft ashore. Roosevelt leaped out lightly and ran for shelter of bushes where he could cover the others as they tied up. That done, he turned and ran toward the campfire.

"Hands up!" he shouted. The man by the fire obeyed.

"Where are the others?" Roosevelt called.

"Hunting. We got to have food," the man said sullenly.

Will guarded him while Roosevelt and Bill crouched by the riverbank, waiting. Wind howled. Cold was intense. Near twilight the other two returned. Roosevelt waited till they were near. Then he rose and shouted, "Hands up!" The men surrendered. The chase had ended — but the serious troubles had only begun.

The bitter cold made prisoners a problem. Tied, hands and feet would freeze. So Roosevelt wrapped their guns in bedding and roped the bundles tightly. Prisoners were lightly bound and Roosevelt, from twenty feet away, stood guard where he had room for action if anyone moved. Bill got wood; Will cooked deer meat.

After the prisoners slept, the Elkhorn men conferred.

"Westerners would have shot them before supper," Will said, warming his hands over the coals.

"How far to a sheriff?" Bill asked.

"A hundred miles, maybe more," Roosevelt answered. "But we have no choice. We have to turn them over to the law."

Through storm and blizzard, the last part of the two-weeks' journey on foot, Roosevelt, Sewall, and Dow made that journey. They fed six, made fires, guarded prisoners night and day. All were haggard when they finally turned the thieves over to the sheriff at Dickinson, the nearest town.

"Why did you bother?" a cowboy exclaimed when, a month later, the men got home. "You coulda shot 'em right off."

Roosevelt pondered his answer.

"Soon these ranches will be gone. Homesteaders will come, and they will expect a law-abiding community. This was a good time to make a start."

The cowboy flicked his chaps with his quirt and turned away, only half understanding.

"The boss is a queer one," he said, "but I like him."

Call to Action

Spring and summer of 1886 passed with the usual round of ranch activities. Roosevelt's cattle business was not yet profitable, but the herds promised well. Shipments of beeves East increased, and he hoped that soon his venture would be a financial success.

One warm September day, Roosevelt sat on the veranda of Elkhorn ranch house and unfolded a New York newspaper. A headline seemed to leap at him from the front page:

"Theodore Roosevelt considered as nominee for Mayor of New York City."

He dropped the paper, and for a moment his favorite rocking chair was quiet as he looked across the Little Missouri River. Sandbars gleamed in the bottoms; the meadow beyond showed a tinge of green in spite of the long heat. High on the sheer cliffs lay a grassy plain where cattle grazed. Hermit-thrushes, thrashers, and meadow larks sang — not gaily as in the spring, but pleasantly. It would be hard to leave this place.

Here he had learned to ride the herds, to hunt for food, to take toil and hardship without complaint. The newcomer, intrigued with cowboy finery, was now in his twenty-eighth year and had grown to be a hard-muscled, courageous man whose shabby clothes were weather-worn — and he did not care. Now, Theodore Roosevelt could ride forty hours with only a pause to change horses; he could endure heat and cold, fierce sun and bitter wind along with men who had long followed that way of life. He had learned to understand the cowboy's creed: "Never show a gun unless you are ready to shoot." His reward was the earned respect and the friendship of the men around him.

Roosevelt turned from the view, called Bill Sewall, and told him the news.

"I've always known, in the back of my mind, that my time here was limited, Bill. I've known that this whole ranch life, as it is now, is only a phase in the opening of the West. America is a country of small homes. Thomas Jefferson believed that, and he was right. These huge ranches will be broken up; homestead farms will be fenced in. I'm glad I got here when I did and that you were with me. Life here teaches a man self-reliance and quick decision; I'll need both." He paused and listened to a thrush.

"Got any plans, Mr. Roosevelt?" Bill asked quietly.

"Maybe you and Will can run Elkhorn Ranch for me? I'd better sell the Maltese Cross Ranch if a chance comes. I'll take the train for New York tomorrow." He rocked silently for a minute, then rose briskly and went inside. There was much to be done before he left.

And so, suddenly, the East called him back. But the West and all it had taught him of work, and friends, and his country, went with him. Memories of these would ever be cherished in his mind and heart.

On the train he thought over the political situation in his home city. He had followed it with keen interest ever since he had served on that Committee of Cities in the Assembly. Tammany was in a difficult spot in '86 and had decided on virtue, for the moment. They nominated Abraham Hewitt, a good conservative, who would attract votes.

Papers had told of the United Labor Party's plan to make Henry George their candidate. George was a fine man, a social philosopher, whose new plan for government revenue known as the "Single Tax" attracted a large following. Many who studied Henry George's writing approved his ideas. They felt he offered real hope for the poor.

When Roosevelt arrived in New York, he threw himself into political work. In October Republicans nominated him for

mayor, and soon he was endorsed by the Independents. He
made speeches and worked hard in the three-way battle for
votes. But he and Henry George were defeated. Hewitt had
half again as many votes as Roosevelt, who ran third. Newspapers announced that this defeat ended his political future.

Roosevelt never wasted energy on regrets, especially now,
when a new joy came into his life. His childhood acquaintance
with his sister's favorite friend, Edith Carow, had suddenly revived as romantic love. He followed her to England, and in
December they were quietly married in London.

After a few months of travel they came home and settled
in a roomy house that Roosevelt had built on Sagamore Hill, at
Oyster Bay. The view from their hilltop was wide and beautiful;
woods, meadows and the Cove provided sports they both enjoyed. Roosevelt settled down happily to writing, spaced with
vigorous exercise and occasional trips to Dakota. It was a good
life, and he enjoyed it.

Two short biographies were followed by *Ranch Life and
The Hunting Trail* which was reviewed in *Forest and Stream,* a
magazine of the outdoors. Roosevelt was pleased and his call
on the editor, George Bird Grinnell, was the beginning of a close
friendship between the two men. That autumn, Roosevelt invited Grinnell and a few others to dine at his home; they
organized a Boone and Crockett Club with their host as the first
president. This club determined to promote manly sport, encourage travel and exploring, study habits of wild animals, and
foster laws for conservation of birds, fish, and game. All this
was a big undertaking. But Roosevelt showed unsuspected abil-

ity in presenting ideas, and soon many such clubs were organized over the nation. It was a novel hobby for that time.

Meanwhile the cattle business was not prospering. The winter the Roosevelts were in Europe was the coldest in the memory of Dakota settlers. Cattle died by thousands from starvation and bitter cold. Roosevelt's losses were heavy. The need for income spurred him to diligent writing; some of it too hurried, some excellent. He began a several-volume work of history, *The Winning of the West*, which was years growing and which ranked along with his *Naval History of the War of 1812*.

Each of these years Roosevelt went out to Elkhorn Ranch to attend to its business, and to hunt. It was on one of these hunting trips that he had his closest brush with death by a wild animal.

A guide always went along, and heretofore they had been agreeable, skilled men. This one was lazy, incompetent, and scornful of a tenderfoot and a Four-eyes. As they swung around four or five days from home, Roosevelt decided to break away. He left provisions and rode on alone. Quiet was welcome after so much quarrelsome talk.

The next day as he hunted grouse for supper, he happened upon a huge grizzly bear, erect and angry in the twilight. Roosevelt fired.

As the wounded bear backed into the thicket, his fierce growls were enough to chill the heart of the bravest hunter. Boldly Roosevelt followed him, shooting again — but still he did not kill him.

Suddenly the bear charged. His wounds gave him an un-

certain gait, and it was difficult to aim in the dim light. Smoke
hung heavy; the roar of shots was stupefying. Close to his eyes
Roosevelt saw a mighty paw, reaching out —

With a boxer's instinct, he dodged in time. The wounded
bear, that paw still twitching angrily, collapsed on the very spot
where Roosevelt had stood.

Night was falling. Hastily he unsheathed his knife, skinned

the bear and loaded the bloody hide on the pack pony. He could not take the carcass, and it would be dangerous to camp near; the scent of freshly killed meat might already be drawing wolves, cougars, or more bears. He had to get away — and fast.

Killing that bear was a real feat. But before Roosevelt got back to the ranch, killing it seemed easy compared with transporting the hide. However he packed the thing it slid off his pony! The folded skin would ride a couple of hundred feet, then ooze like hot mush between the carefully tied ropes. By the time that three-day journey ended, Roosevelt felt that he had earned his bearskin twice, killing and hauling. But it was a beauty, and he was proud to take it back East.

Roosevelt took an active part in the presidential campaign of 1888, when General Harrison was elected over Cleveland. Naturally, he thought Harrison might want him in a federal office, perhaps in the State Department. But Blaine was appointed secretary and did not want a man who had worked against him in the '84 convention.

Shortly after his inauguration, President Harrison appointed Roosevelt to be one of the three Civil Service Commissioners. This was a logical appointment because Roosevelt had worked for Civil Service in New York State. But friends thought the job was not important.

"You shouldn't take that post," a friend advised. "It has no future. You'll be buried in detail."

"I've already heard that," Roosevelt chuckled. "The New York papers are pleased. They are delighted that I'll be buried — outside New York!"

"Maybe they don't know you!" The friend left, grinning. Come to think of it, Theodore would be hard to bury!

The post really was not flattering and it paid only $3,500 a year. But Roosevelt went at once to take it. He breezed into the office on a May morning.

"I'm the new commissioner," he announced to the astonished clerk, and began giving orders. When he met the other commissioners, he saw they were men of high character and little initiative. The department ran as one man — Roosevelt.

The idea back of Civil Service, though not that name, was introduced by Thomas Jefferson. John Adams had lost the election of 1800, but he boldly appointed scores of men to federal office before he left the presidency. When Jefferson began his term he refused to dismiss Adams men unless they were incompetent.

Roosevelt promptly made his view clear.

"Patronage does not help a party," he said. "The most sweeping victories in our history have been won against it. Patronage does help the worst element in a party.

"Our kind of government has two dangers: good citizens are not always active and the other kind are *always* active."

The first move was to enforce the law on the books. With another commissioner, Roosevelt went to New York to visit the Customs House. They found so much fraud that they demanded the removal of three employees and the prosecution of one. This served notice that the commissioner meant business.

Soon they decided to visit several other cities. Reporters came to the train to see them off.

"We plan to accomplish two things," Roosevelt told them. "Make officials understand that the law must be obeyed and get that same idea into citizens' heads!"

There were many meetings and speeches. The flair for publicity Roosevelt had developed for the Boone and Crockett Club was a help now. His speaking won attention; he had a way of turning out a phrase that newspapers liked to quote and that people remembered. He saw to it, always, that newspapers had his version of a story. All this helped to get good newspaper reports.

A thousand difficulties developed, for senators and congressmen did not like to give up their power to dole out jobs. Roosevelt established stiff competitive examinations for each and every position under Civil Service. The federal legislators ridiculed these and often prevented them from being held.

Roosevelt did not think that examinations were perfect.

"I concede that when we want a man, out West, in a job that needs a rifleman, it is silly to examine his spelling. We are trying to improve our tests all the time; but, even now, this is a better way to select a man than to appoint him merely for his vote." He asked for a better method, and no one made a suggestion. The rank and file of citizens approved what he was doing; that encouraged him. Perhaps the greatest good accomplished was the changed feeling of the people about the spoils of politics. No magical transformation took place; Civil Service was far from perfect. But people thereafter would be a little suspicious of political patronage. It would be a long time, if ever, before that evil would dare be as bold as it had been.

The years in Washington were happy ones for the Roosevelt family. Alice was five and Theodore, junior, two when the move was made. Kermit, Ethel, and Archie were born while the family lived in the modest house off Connecticut Avenue. Outings were enjoyed in Rock Creek Park. They drove out to the park in the carriage, taking with them a small wooden wagon. On the walk, the younger ones who wearied of tramping could get a lift now and then.

Mornings the children hurried to their father's room to visit while he dressed. He kept a small box on his dresser, a ditty-box they called it. In it were wonderful treasures — a few things from Grandfather Theodore's own box, a feather from an Egyptian bird, a tooth from that grizzly, a bullet that had killed a coyote out West.

"Tell us about this," Kermit said, the morning it was his turn to choose.

"Oh, that," Roosevelt paused in pulling on his shoes. "That's a bit of beading from the first buckskin shirt I had. Did I tell you about that?" He had, but they always wanted the tale again. By the time it ended, the bell rang for breakfast, and they dashed downstairs together.

The Roosevelts had many friends. They entertained simply, usually at Sunday tea; dinners were too expensive. Richard Harding Davis, the newspaper correspondent, and Rudyard Kipling were frequent guests, along with William Howard Taft and Henry Adams.

Mrs. Roosevelt and the children spent the summers at Oyster Bay, and Mr. Roosevelt came up as often as he could leave

his work. The place was named Sagamore Hill, after the chief
of an Indian tribe that had once lived on that part of Long Island.
The house was a big rambling frame building of more than
twenty rooms. Gardens supplied most of the food for the family
and countless guests — relatives, friends of various ages, and
political visitors — all of whom were promptly taken into the gay
and happy informalities of family life.

Roosevelt himself chopped trees to clear paths, gardens,
and vistas, and otherwise got his exercise by riding, water sports,

or tramps — always with the children in tow. He had the gift for being one of them — perhaps because he never tried. It was simply natural to him.

Roosevelt wrote each afternoon while at Sagamore Hill, and finished *The Winning of the West*. The fine reviews written about it were very gratifying. The sale, fortunately, was good. The added income was a very welcome help toward the expenses of a growing family. Theodore Roosevelt was not rich.

At the end of six years, Roosevelt began to feel a little stale on the job. His very success in arousing interest in Civil Service made battling for the cause less needed as time went by. He was beginning to wonder what to do next when, in the spring of 1895, the Mayor offered him the job of Police Commissioner of New York City. Roosevelt promptly accepted the task.

That should be a real opportunity for a fighter.

Haroun-al-Roosevelt

The government of New York City had interested Theodore Roosevelt from the time he joined the Twenty-first Ward Republican Club the year he graduated from Harvard. Defeat for the office of mayor did not kill that interest. He kept well informed about the city's fortunes and misfortunes all the years he lived in Washington.

This interest in the city made him notice a new book published in 1890, written by Jacob Riis, a reporter on a New York newspaper. *How the Other Half Lives* fascinated him. It opened new vistas to his mind and heart much as spectacles had opened the physical world to his eyes. Suddenly he began to understand the terrible meaning of poverty.

"Imagine! I thought that clean cigars and health of smokers were important when that bill was up in the legislature!" In a fury of self-disgust, he closed the book and paced the floor of their sitting room. His wife looked up in surprise.

"Blind that I was! Listen to this, Edith!" He read several pages that had stirred him.

"But what can you do about it, Theodore?" she asked. She was a tender-hearted, kind person, quick to help anyone in need. But the picture the book revealed was so huge, so shocking! It seemed remote, impersonal; not like poverty one could see and know in one's neighborhood.

"Do? We could enforce law. We could make *better* laws. We could see that people have a fair chance to make a decent living. What must these newcomers think of America — of *us,* when they find life so different from their dreams? They are swamped in the squalor they do not understand!"

Roosevelt finished the book. He made inquiries about the author and found that Jacob Riis was a Danish-born immigrant now working on a New York newspaper, and that his story of tenement-house life was true. He learned that one-third of all the babies born there died in their first year; that 50,000 dirty, hungry children roamed filthy streets because there was no place else for them to be. Schools were over-crowded even without these newcomers.

In his inquiries Roosevelt chanced to learn of another person who was also aware of human needs. He discovered that Jane Addams, in Chicago, had opened Hull House for the very kind of people Jacob Riis had written of in New York.

"If I ever have a chance — " he had vowed to himself. Now, with Mayor Strong's appointment, that chance had come. Roosevelt resigned his position as Civil Service Commissioner and took his family to New York. Hundreds protested; said he should not leave work that was going well. But Roosevelt was firm. He felt sure that under a non-partisan mayor of Strong's integrity he could do useful work in New York City.

Roosevelt's office was in Police Headquarters, in a dingy, vermin-infested building on Mulberry Street. The place had changed little — and that for the worse — since he had visited there during his terms as a legislator. At once he told the other commissioners about his plans.

"First," he pounded his right fist on his left palm, "we shall enforce the law. Second, we shall use full publicity. Third, we shall pay no heed to partisan politics."

The commissioners smilingly agreed. Two of the three were against Roosevelt, but they had decided to keep their opposition secret; give a man enough rope and he will hang himself, was their theory.

A very short time after he took office, Roosevelt was looking over records of the department when word was brought in of a dramatic rescue. An older policeman, veteran of the Civil War, had plunged into the river and rescued a drowning woman.

"What's his record?" Roosevelt asked, turning pages.

"He's saved twenty-eight lives all told," the man who had

brought the news answered quickly. "Got two medals from Congress. But medals buy no clothes."

"What do you mean by that?" Roosevelt looked up, puzzled.

"He ruined his suit, sir. New ones cost money. And it ain't the first time, either. His beat's along the river, and that's bad for uniforms. He really can't afford to rescue, but he keeps right on doing it."

"Doesn't the city replace his uniform?" demanded the new commissioner, his eyes beginning to flash.

"Why, no, sir. It isn't done. Look at that man who stopped the run-away on Park Avenue. Saved three lives but broke his legs and tore his uniform to shreds. He was laid off a long time and with a family he can't afford that."

"And they didn't — they didn't — " Roosevelt sputtered.

"No, sir. No more did they when that man's brother carried three out of a burning building. Of course *his* uniform was ruined, too. Seems like there are some men on this force haven't sense to look after their own good."

Roosevelt stood up hastily and pounded on his blotter.

"We're going to change that! Now! Hear me! A man who loses a uniform protecting citizens gets a new one from the city of New York! Legs broken in the city's work are the city's business."

News of that order seeped out through the force. Soon after came the announcement that promotions, hereafter, would be made on merit, not "pull." Incredulous policemen felt a new pride in their work; every man who walked a beat was encouraged to do his best.

Reporters flocked to interview Roosevelt. He had a flair for turning daily routine into pungent news. He focused public attention upon the slums; for the first time citizens thought of the need for schools and playgrounds to keep children off city streets.

But graft, one of the fundamental evils in the city government, was not so easy to dramatize. However, Roosevelt determined to try.

A city law required that saloons should close on Sunday. It had passed in a period of reform; respectable people liked the idea of having it on the books, though they did nothing further to support it.

"The timid good are a menace to our form of government," Roosevelt remarked to a reporter. "By that I mean, people who think of themselves as good citizens but lack courage to fight. Reform does not come by words; only action gets results. Lincoln had a word for the timid. He called them 'silk stocking reformers.' Inertia of 'good' citizens is one of the gravest dangers in America." Roosevelt felt strongly about citizens who did not support laws they had made.

Actually, corrupt politicians liked that Sunday closing law; they made money by it. They collected graft, in cash, from saloon keepers and in return policemen ignored side-doors where customers came and went freely all the Sabbath Day. Saloon keepers who refused to pay were annoyed and often taken to court on trumped-up offenses. All this was no secret. It was simply ignored by common consent.

Of course Sunday closing was not the only way of extorting

money for law-violation; gambling, vice, obstructions on streets and sidewalks were among the many profitable sources of income for the higher-ups. But Sunday closing was so obvious that Roosevelt resolved to begin his campaign for law and order with it. He announced his plan and was met head-on with fury.

"You can't do that!" men shouted at him.

"You'll be ruined! Sunday closing is an old law; you have to enforce it with discretion."

"I took the oath of office," Roosevelt answered quietly. "I promised to uphold the law. I don't recall that the oath mentioned 'discretion.'"

Men growled at his stupidity.

"Perhaps we should let Abraham Lincoln speak here," Roosevelt said, and quoted from one of the great man's speeches:

"'Let every American remember that to violate the law is to tear the charter out of his own and his children's liberty. Let reverence for the law be taught in schools and in colleges; let it be written in primers, spelling books, and almanacs; let it be preached from the pulpit, proclaimed in the legislative halls and enforced in the courts of justice. Let it become the political religion of the land.'"

Silenced for the moment, those men saw that they could not oppose Roosevelt openly. So they set to work slyly, behind his back. They tried to trip him with personal scandal and found none. They told reporters that he took policemen off regular beats to guard saloons and that crime increased. Hundreds of false rumors were whispered around.

Roosevelt seemed to be the only calm man at Headquarters.

No matter what the turmoil, he always had an occasional light
touch. In the heat of that summer he appeared on Mulberry
Street without a vest — a sartorial crisis in the 1890's! Instead
of the hot vest, he wore a cummerbund, a kind of sash, wrapped
twice around his waist with ends hanging down. The fringe
showed below his coat. The sash was cooler than a vest; he
enjoyed wearing it.

That same summer Roosevelt began taking midnight walks
in the tenement districts. With Jacob Riis, now his devoted
friend, he wandered down alleys, up rickety stairs, along dark
streets. When the weather was cool enough, Roosevelt wore a
dark cloak that was somewhat of a disguise.

The purpose, he said, was to discover whether policemen were actually on duty. When an officer of the law was discovered asleep or loafing in a saloon instead of walking his beat, Roosevelt promptly made himself known.

"Those white teeth flashed out at me — it was the Head himself!" faithless officers protested.

When news of the midnight walks got around, newspaper cartoons showed the Police Commissioner flashing exaggerated white teeth at trembling policemen. The dangling sash, the eyeglasses, the teeth, fairly invited cartoons. Reporters coined the picturesque name Haroun-al-Roosevelt for him, a parody on the name of the famous caliph who disguised himself and wandered through the streets of Bagdad in the tales of the thousand and one Arabian nights.

People laughed; but the whole thing had little humor to policemen who faced the Head in the cool light of the morning after. Roosevelt could come back to the office, sleep an hour, get his coffee and be ready for a day's law-enforcement. His physical endurance amazed the force.

All this was news. But to the night walkers, Riis and Roosevelt, their rambles had a far deeper meaning than merely checking policemen. Riis was giving Roosevelt an education in the needs of Americans. As part of his office, Roosevelt was also on the Board of Health, and Riis believed that if he knew facts about the needs of the poor, he might be able to help them. Riis knew that they did not want charity — not those sturdy souls who had braved the journey across the Atlantic to reach the country of their dreams. They did need an honest, friendly hand and a chance to learn the language and new ways. Then they could stand on their own feet in the new land.

In September of '95 politicians thought it smart to organize a parade in defiance of Roosevelt. State elections were coming on; the favorable write-ups Riis and a few others were giving Roosevelt must be checked. The public must be shown that the man's efforts were quite trivial. Elaborate preparations were made, and some daring soul made the mistake of inviting Roosevelt to see his own undoing.

To the committee's horror and astonishment Roosevelt enjoyed the whole thing. He laughed when a coffin labeled "Teddyism" was solemnly carried by. He chuckled at placards bearing strange phrases. He roared at one which asked "Have you ever seen Roosevelt's name in print?" This when that name was in newspaper headlines almost every day.

Hundreds roared with him when a marcher shouted in German, "Where is this Roosevelt!"

"Here I am!" Roosevelt leaned over and shouted back — in German. New York papers the next morning gave detailed stories of incidents of that parade. Instead of being crushed, Roosevelt enjoyed it, and his following was strengthened.

Through all the opposition and badgering, Roosevelt held grimly to his plan: obey the law or change it. When men saw that he meant what he said, they changed the law. A new law made it legal to sell liquor "with a meal." A mere pretzel was interpreted as a "meal." Scores of new "hotels" and "restaurants" opened — free from the Sunday closing law.

More disappointments were to come. Roosevelt was sad-

dened when Mayor Strong, on whom he had counted, asked him
to "soften his blows." Two members of the Police Commission
joined together to block every move he could make. The governor, when appealed to, refused his help.

Roosevelt continued to fight for better government, and
he saw some gains. He had made citizens think about their city
and its people. He showed them that if they really wanted
honest government they could have it by voting for honest men.
But wanting good government was more than just wishing for it.
Citizens can get what they *want* — with votes.

"A vote is like a rifle," Roosevelt remarked to Riis. "Its usefulness depends upon the man who uses it."

As months went by, twenty-five hundred policemen were
added to the force by civil service examinations. That method
worked no magic. But it was better for the honor of the force
than getting new men by political appointment. The policemen
liked Roosevelt; they trusted him, and knew he would stand by
every honest man on the force — and get rid of a dishonest one
as soon as he found him.

Early in 1896 the excitement of an important national campaign turned attention from Theodore Roosevelt. Other men
made headlines. Tammany sighed and relaxed. At last they
had stopped that Commissioner Roosevelt!

"Why don't you go out for some other office?" a friend asked
him late that spring. "You could get anything."

"No, you are mistaken," Roosevelt answered. "I shall never
hold another office. I have liked my work here. It has brought
me in touch with all kinds of people, and I enjoy that. I have

had a glimpse of the real life of swarming millions, and I may have helped them a little.

"But I have offended so many 'interests,' antagonized so many politicians, that my future usefulness is ended. What I did was honest — but I am finished."

Apparently it did not occur to Theodore Roosevelt that in this hard and thankless job he had grown in stature; had gained practical knowledge and spiritual understanding. He had struggled to manage a police department and to make a better city. He refused to compromise with evil; but he had learned to work with all kinds of men. This was a gain; but he was too discouraged to realize that.

"I'm thirty-seven years old," he said to his wife, "and I have reached the end of a career in work I love. I wonder what I should do."

"You will find something, Theodore," she answered with confidence. "And when it comes, you will do it well."

The U.S. Navy

The last decade of the nineteenth century came to be known as the "Gay Nineties," but those years were not gay for many thousands of Americans. A depression that began in 1893 lasted five years, and the country suffered from many troubles.

Thousands of immigrants, drawn to the United States by a vision of freedom and better living, crowded into city slums. Farmers could not sell their crops, and in despair joined the futile hunt for jobs in cities and towns.

Nor were the hardships confined to eastern cities. Western farmers and stockmen and thousands of miners were in difficult straits. Silver mines had attracted thousands of workers to the West; now the mines were closed for lack of a market for the metal. Hungry people everywhere looked to leaders for action.

These tragedies had been ignored by both major political parties. The Haymarket bombing in Chicago, the Homestead riot in Pittsburgh, the Pullman strike, and other labor troubles, had been "kept out of politics." Minor parties had risen from time to time since the Civil War, but none was vigorous enough to live. Major parties stupidly repeated the same old evasive campaign issues at every election.

In 1896, with the nation seething underneath, Republicans nominated Major William McKinley for president. Democrats pushed aside Cleveland, twice a president, to nominate William Jennings Bryan, a young lawyer from the Middle West. Bryan was not handsome or learned, but he was endowed with one of the most beautiful voices of all time. His gift for speaking had been discovered when he was a student at Illinois College, and by 1896 he had learned to use it mightily.

The party platforms, as well as the candidates, were bitterly contested at both conventions; "silver" men and "gold" men were in each. "Silver" became an emotional issue almost as intense as the word "slavery" once had been. Silver men said that since there was so much of the metal, the government should freely make it into dollars and get it into circulation — much as the government had printed paper money during Civil War times. The gold men shouted that this flood of dollars would bring on disastrous inflation. But that warning did not frighten people whose pockets were empty and whose debts on homes and farms were unpaid. Free silver would mean more money around; that seemed good.

Businessmen were appalled. Easterners dreaded inflation, and they did not fancy carrying heavy silver dollars with them. They declared that the country should keep the gold standard: that is, keep the law that set the exact amount and quality of gold for each United States dollar.

The convention battles ended with the Republicans standing for the gold standard and the Democrats coming out for free minting of silver in the ratio of 16 ounces of silver to 1 ounce of gold coined. This phrase, 16 to 1, became the battle cry of the campaign. Thousands who had no knowledge of economics shouted it hopefully, thinking of it as some magic code which would bring them easier living.

As the campaign got under way, great meetings were held by both parties. Bands played Sousa's newest marches, and often the great band-leader was there in person, nattily swinging his baton in exquisite rhythm.

When Bryan spoke at the Democrats' rallies, his voice flowed over crowds like organ music, or dropped to a whisper that moved listeners to unashamed tears. The disgruntled, the poor, the jobless, flocked to hear him. *What* he said did not matter. His voice stirred hope among the hopeless. He never tired; he could make forty speeches a day and still that rich voice flowed on.

Frightened Republicans gathered all their forces.

"How about asking Theodore to get out and speak?" someone wondered in desperation.

"Dare we? He has offended so many in the party!"

"Just plain tactless, I call him!"

"But people listen to him. He gets in the news. Look how he turned that parade to his own good last summer. I'm wiring him, asking him to help us."

Roosevelt was reading the telegram in his office when a reporter dropped in. He handed the message to his caller.

"They don't really want me," he said grimly.

"They need you. The campaign is not doing well."

"And it is the most important campaign since 1860. I'm no economist, but common sense tells me that flooding the country with cheap money will not help our poor. I might know as much as Bryan. Since they ask me, I'll pitch in and help."

The reporter grinned and dashed off to write his story.

So Roosevelt began campaigning. Mulberry Street felt little change by his absence because New York politicians had tied his hands with new laws and red tape.

Large audiences listened to Roosevelt's speeches on national needs, and on the gold standard. They approved his honesty and were moved by his patriotic fervor.

Major McKinley was elected by a comfortable margin.

Roosevelt had thought this result would make him very happy. But as he went back to Mulberry Street he was surprised to feel curiously discouraged. Police headquarters were so dingy, and his efforts there now so futile. His situation seemed worse by contrast with the stirring scenes he had so recently shared.

Some federal office would surely give him a better chance for service. Several friends suggested a post in the Navy Department. His fourteen-year-old naval history was still the standard work. His interest in navy matters had continued; surely he would be useful there, they said.

In April of 1897, President McKinley appointed Roosevelt to be Assistant Secretary of the Navy. He had hesitated long because New York politicians were against the man. And, too, the President liked peace and quiet; he feared he would have neither with his new appointee. Roosevelt, McKinley recalled, was thirty-eight, strong as an ox, and had vast energy.

"John Long is quiet and dependable," McKinley said of his Secretary of the Navy. "He will keep Theodore in the background." The friend to whom he spoke smiled doubtfully.

On his part, Roosevelt felt no hesitation. He resigned his

New York position and moved to Washington.

News of his departure shocked New Yorkers. Too late, many rallied to tell him of their interest and to promise support. Hundreds urged him to reconsider and stay there.

"You have only begun to work for honest government!"

"The work you have been doing is the greatest task any American can undertake. Stay and finish."

Testimonial dinners were given; columns filled the newspapers. But Roosevelt would not turn back; not even when reporters predicted that Tammany would return in a year.

"They will never dare be quite so bold again," one newspaper man said. "Let the people glimpse honest government and rogues must be more careful."

Several Washington newspapers pointed out that the new appointment was wise for the nation; few men knew the needs of the navy as Theodore Roosevelt did. One paper that had often opposed him on Civil Service work spoke now in praise of his courage, honesty, and hatred of meanness.

"Perhaps a little stirring up will be good for us," the article ended.

Soon Roosevelt went to inspect navy yards, torpedo boats, and various ships. The report he promptly turned in was as exciting reading as his books.

On the second of June, Roosevelt made a carefully prepared address at the Naval War College, Newport. It was printed in many newspapers and gave all Americans, as well as navy men, a chance to know his views. Many remembered whole sentences and quoted them often.

"A century has passed since Washington wrote 'To be prepared for war is the most effectual means to promote peace.' We pay to this maxim the lip-loyalty we so often pay to Washington's words; but it has never sunk deep into our hearts."

"In this country there is not the slightest danger of an over-development of warlike spirit, and there never has been any such danger. . . . The danger is precisely the opposite . . . we can only secure peace by being ready and willing to fight for it."

"Preparation for war is the surest guarantee for peace."

"It is too late to prepare for war when the time of peace has passed."

"No nation should wage war wantonly; nor fight unless forced to; but it should always be ready to fight."

"Every feat of heroism makes us forever indebted to the man who performed it."

Most newspapers praised this address. They called it "manly," "patriotic," "inspiring to the youth of America." One Washington paper said that Roosevelt honored himself and his country by his appeal for a stronger navy.

Many times since the Civil War, dangerous world events might have made Americans think about their navy — and didn't. But that summer of 1897, Roosevelt's words caught public attention because of what was going on in Cuba.

Some years earlier, Cuban patriots had begun a revolt against Spain and her mistreatment of the natives. As the revolution grew it did harm to American, as well as Cuban, sugar plantations. Yellow fever was a scourge on the island and spread unchecked to Florida and the Gulf states. Spain boldly killed countless Cubans by starvation and guerrilla warfare — all so near the shores of freedom-loving America.

People in the United States felt sorry about all this; some, remembering the American struggle for freedom, had sympathy for the Cuban patriots. But Americans were not ready for war, either in their minds or with their army and navy. So the matter drifted; nothing was done.

Roosevelt saw that the situation was dangerous and felt it was his duty to see that ships were built. The navy had wonderful officers and men, but because of public indifference after the Civil War, it had lost vigor. The new Assistant Secretary meant to overcome that indifference. He was so successful that some thought he went too far. There was considerable talk about him.

"That Roosevelt will get us into war if he keeps on!"

"I don't think Theodore is making a war," one of his friends said during an argument. "But I think it would not be a bad idea if he did. Have you read the latest dispatches?" Newspapers printed many reports about Spanish atrocities in Cuba. The shocking situation was not a secret.

"Roosevelt might welcome war because he would have a good cause to defend," a man who knew him said.

"Teddy'd be in the thick of it," someone remarked. The friend turned; that man marked himself as a stranger to Mr. Roosevelt. His friends never called him "Teddy" — he hated that nickname the public had coined for him.

Five months after he took office he gave Secretary Long a detailed list of the number and kind of ships needed in case of war. Men who said Roosevelt was all bluster should have seen that practical and explicit document.

During this time he discovered that navy gunners had not been allowed enough money for training in target practice. He ordered nearly a million dollars for training in the new precision marksmanship. Some men raged at the "waste"!

"Did you hear what Roosevelt's up to now? He's letting them shoot money into the sea."

Roosevelt was calm when he heard that. "We have a new type of gun since the Civil War," he reminded critics. "Our men must learn to use it. In war, you know, the only shots that count are the ones that hit."

In these studies, too, he came upon an internal dispute that was causing needless friction inside the navy. As years passed and new ships were built, jealousies grew between officers of the line and engineers. Almost every ship had aboard men from the two hostile groups. Roosevelt ordered that all cadets must have training as line officers *and* engineers. In the future, an officer would know not only how to command a ship but how to repair a damaged engine.

In January Roosevelt sent a formal letter to Long, giving him the exact location of every American ship. Later in that month the American consul in Cuba asked for an American ship to stand by at Havana to protect American interests. The battleship *Maine* was sent at once.

Then during the night of February 15th, the *Maine* blew up in the harbor at Havana; two officers and some 260 men were killed. Everyone, from the President to the man on the street, was inflamed with anger.

"Now McKinley will *have* to declare war!" people cried.

Most Americans believed that Spain had ordered the *Maine's* destruction. Actually, it was not known whether Spain did so order; whether an internal explosion was the cause; or whether a Cuban fanatic was responsible for the disaster.

As for Roosevelt, he felt sure that war was near. When it came, he wanted the navy to be ready for action. Spain's fleets were divided. One was near the Canary Islands ready to sail to Puerto Rico; the other was at Manila in the Philippines, where it could harass the United States West Coast.

The American Asiatic fleet was in Hong Kong. On a day when Secretary Long was at home, Roosevelt cabled its commodore, George Dewey, ordering him to keep his ships in full supply and keep them together.

On the 19th of April, already an historic day for Americans, Congress passed important resolutions. It declared that Cuba's independence was recognized; that Congress would use force to help if necessary; and that when a firm, independent government was assured, the United States would withdraw. Europe laughed in derision at that last — but the United States faithfully carried out her pledge.

On the 25th of April, Congress declared war on Spain. Dewey was ordered to proceed to Manila and destroy or capture the Spanish Fleet. *Because he was ready,* he reached Manila on the 30th; his flagship was a mile beyond the great rock, Corregidor, before the United States fleet was discovered.

Firing began and, because of the fleet's fine marksmanship, was disastrous to the enemy. Spaniards ran up the white flag at noon. American casualties were light.

This same week Theodore Roosevelt resigned his navy post and volunteered as a soldier. Many personal reasons might have kept Roosevelt from this action; his fourth son, Quentin, was only a few months old, and Mrs. Roosevelt had been very ill. His six children needed their good father, and he was useful in his navy position.

"Why do you volunteer?" friends asked him.

"I like life," he answered thoughtfully; "I have no spirit of reckless exhilaration. But I have an interest in Cuba and her urge for freedom from oppression. I find it easier to explain to my children why I go than why I would not go. When a man believes something is right he must be willing to back his faith with his body — I can do no less."

They could not persuade him to stay at home.

Congress ordered the raising of three volunteer Cavalry Regiments and Secretary of War Alger offered command of one to Roosevelt. "I'll make you colonel of the First U.S. Volunteer Cavalry; the nation will like that," the Secretary said.

"I can't be colonel," Roosevelt said. "I've had no training except in the National Guard, years ago. Make Leonard Wood colonel. I'll serve under him as lieutenant colonel. I'll study hard and learn drills and such. But Wood already knows how to manage a regiment. Time is important, now."

"But why should you serve under Wood — or anyone?" Alger asked. "Let him do the work; I'll make you colonel."

"No man does my work for me," Roosevelt exclaimed. "Wood will have to do the work; Wood shall have the title. That's settled. When may we start?"

Alger smiled and agreed on an early date.

Roosevelt sent off letters to start the recruiting. He ordered a uniform from New York, bought a horse in Texas, and got himself twelve pairs of steel-rimmed spectacles. Wood had gone on to San Antonio where the regiment was to train.

On the day Roosevelt left Washington, Jacob Riis went to the station to see him off. They talked little — what was there to say? Roosevelt was doing what he thought was right, and Riis respected him for his courage.

As the train pulled out of the station Riis stared after it. Suddenly he wondered, would his friend return? One thing was certain, Roosevelt would not spare himself.

The Rough Riders

Roosevelt's call for volunteers to drive the Spaniards out of Cuba drew a motley lot of men to San Antonio. Ranchmen, cowboys, hunters, who had known Roosevelt in the West, were joined by gamblers and drifters along the border. They rode their own horses and carried their excellent firearms.

From the East, college men, football heroes, polo-players, sportsmen, and men who wanted adventure arrived in smaller numbers. They brought elegant luggage which they sent to camp, south of the city.

All admired the manly qualities of Theodore Roosevelt; he seemed to typify courage, daring, strength. To a man, they hated a bully and believed that Spain had been bullying Cuba. They wanted to be in the first expedition to right that wrong. Leonard Wood was colonel, but the regiment was Roosevelt's from the beginning.

San Antonio residents were agog over the volunteers. American newspapers, at the moment, were filled with Dewey's success in the Pacific but San Antonians only glanced at headlines. Reckless cowboys, dashing along their streets, were more fascinating.

"Have you seen the latest batch of 'Teddy's Terrors'?" people asked each other after each train arrival.

"Seen 'em? Yes. I've heard 'em, too. I tell my children to stay near the house. Those men are rough riders; they'll be jumping our fences just to show they can!"

Those words, "rough riders," were repeated often. By the time Roosevelt stepped off the train on the 15th of May a great sign hung near the station:

THIS WAY TO ROOSEVELT'S ROUGH RIDER CAMP

He grinned ruefully. At least that name was better than "Teddy's Terrors" of which he had heard by letter.

In suggesting Leonard Wood for Colonel of the First Volunteer Cavalry, Roosevelt had made an excellent choice. Wood, a graduate physician, was an army doctor who had served in western campaigns. He was alert and energetic; had studied hard to add military knowledge to his medical training.

Wood was absorbed in the difficult task of collecting equipment and supplies for the regiment; so when Roosevelt arrived, he quickly turned over the routine drilling. The men bought hundreds of drill manuals and the new lieutenant colonel and his men learned together.

Roosevelt drilled them for hours under the scorching Texas sun — afoot and on horse. Their good humor and high morale astonished regular army officers while their easy comradeship with their lieutenant colonel shocked them.

Most of the Western volunteers were already expert in marksmanship, riding, and care of themselves and their equipment. Untrained men learned fast in such a group.

While volunteers were assembling and training in Texas, people over the nation read about the Rough Riders in their newspapers. Many were scornful.

"I never heard of such doings!" some said.

"Never? Then you forget history," a thoughtful person was sure to answer. "Always in a crisis, men like these have left their daily tasks to help America. They have been daring men; they count the cost and are willing to pay it for liberty and justice. Remember the Texas Rangers?"

"You're right! I had not thought of the Rough Riders that way. Washington had such men when Fort Duquesne was to be taken. Westerners took King's Mountain from the British and volunteers followed George Rogers Clark and Andrew Jackson. America can count on her people in time of need."

"I wish politicians in Washington were equally devoted," someone would remark.

"*We* put those men there — remember?" was the answer.

All the time talk went on, the First U.S. Volunteer Cavalry was drilling under the southern sun, turning a group of individualists into a regiment that could work together. The skill of officers and devotion of the men is proved by the fact that in sixty days the regiment was trained, transported to Cuba, and put in active service. That feat would have been impossible with green recruits; it was not easy with experienced Westerners.

The Rough Riders entrained for Tampa on the 29th of May. They found that place in utter confusion. Officers, men, horses, mules, milled about in each other's way. Food and fodder were scarce. Heavy woolen uniforms arrived for men who were to fight in the tropics. This shocked Roosevelt.

"Why *woolen?*" he cried when he got Wood's attention.

"Just routine!" Wood laughed at Roosevelt's wry expression. "For years the army has been issuing winter uniforms this time of year so that in a nice leisurely way they can be delivered by fall. You can't expect the War Department to change its ways suddenly!" Roosevelt had no patience with the confusion and waste he saw about him.

"The government has known that this war might come!" he exclaimed. "Will they never learn to be ready?"

Colonel Wood shrugged. He knew how hard Roosevelt had tried to make the nation prepare. Many tales about the state of the War Department were passed around at Tampa.

One story quoted a harassed clerk in Washington:

"We had the War Department running so smoothly! Now a war comes along and upsets everything!" The story may have been a fiction but a day at Tampa made it seem probable.

Men grew impatient. Everyone complained.

"The war will be over before we get there!"

"I wanted to shoot a Spaniard or two. Now I wonder if we'll even see an island!" Morale dropped lower each day.

After a week of this Colonel Wood was told to take a motor launch and locate a transport for his regiment. The Rough Riders under Roosevelt entrained for the quay. Presently Roosevelt spied the Colonel on the deck of the *Yucatan* drawing near. He moved his men to the gangplank on the double and there collided with regulars and some volunteers who also had orders to embark. The transport would not hold half those men! Roosevelt resolved that his regiment would not be the one left behind.

He marched right past the volunteers. But regulars were not so easily pushed aside.

"Take your men off!" their colonel sent word.

The *Yucatan* was coming nearer. Roosevelt saw he must gain a bit of time before acting. He replied quietly:

"Tell your colonel that I would like so very much to oblige, but my orders — " This in the suave manner he could assume on occasion. And at the same time he eyed the deck of the *Yucatan*. Colonel Wood was shouting something — words were lost above the crowd. Knowing Wood, Roosevelt felt sure he had shouted an order. At that moment the messenger returned.

"My orders are to board," he told the messenger and gestured toward Wood. "So sorry — " His regiment, grinning gleefully, marched aboard as the gangplank dropped.

Alas! The regulars boarded, too, and even some other volunteers. Soon the transport was so solidly packed that men could not move about. In despair at the over-crowding, the captain returned to the Bay. There they waited one whole week for sailing orders. A miserable week that was, for hot sun shone on the transport anchored in the middle of a stinking stream of sewerage from Tampa. Probably no men were ever so glad to depart for battle as those soldiers when, finally, the transport steamed south.

A heavy sea was rolling, and small boats had trouble landing

at Daiquiri, Cuba. Men were hurt; one was lost. Horses, except for officers', and all mules, had been left behind. Cowboys, used to riding even to a nearby chuck-wagon, now walked miles up the beach — in woolen uniforms.

Why the Spaniards allowed 12,000 or more American troops to land in daylight and with ample noise to make their movement known; why with 190,000 or more Spanish troops on Cuba, the Americans were so quickly victorious, are only two of the scores of unanswered questions about this brief war with Spain.

The regiment reached Siboney in a tropical downpour. When it ended, Rough Riders built fires, dried out as best they could, and shared food some had carried in pockets.

That night orders came from the commander in charge of the expedition. Wood's men were to move at dawn along a hill trail, about four miles, then attack the advance Spanish position. Regulars would march up the valley trail and join them at Las Guasimas, the meeting of two trails.

The terrain was thick jungle on mountains; deep green, dense, and forbidding. Wood and his brown-uniformed troops sighted Spaniards at the very moment shooting began on the valley trail. He sent word to Roosevelt and Major Brodie.

"Deploy your men right and left, alternating. Connect with regulars on the right if possible."

The first troop went right. Brodie took the second, left, and Roosevelt was about to deploy the third, right, when, to his horror, he observed that the first had disappeared into the jungle. Would an officer be court-martialed for losing his troops? The manual had not taught about this!

"I'll stay with the third," Roosevelt said to Richard Harding Davis, his friend and a war correspondent, who happened near. "I'm hunting the firing-line, Davis."

A sudden burst of shooting was deafening.

"You've found it!" Davis said as bullets whizzed. "War is not like people at home imagine, is it?"

"Bullets sound like silk, tearing," Roosevelt said in wonder. "Why! They're shooting at *us!* Lie flat, men! Take shelter if you can!"

He searched with field glasses for the enemy position; smokeless powder gave no clue. "These things are a nuisance with spectacles. What do you make out, Davis?"

"There! Look!" Davis cried. "See those hats?"

Roosevelt focused on a trench about three-quarters of a mile away. He saw figures moving, and the conical hats were certainly not U.S. government issue.

"Advance and fire!" Roosevelt shouted — and hoped this was the right order. The men obeyed. But by the time they reached the trench it was empty.

What to do next was a puzzle. Thick, lush jungle lay around them. Should they stay and hold the position lest Spaniards return? Should they join the regulars — and if so, to the right or left? Roosevelt was sure on only one point; he should keep his doubts to himself. His men depended on him; he must act promptly to find what was expected.

With two orderlies to bring back messages, Roosevelt set out to explore. By good luck, he came upon Colonel Wood.

"You did right," Wood approved when Roosevelt had reported. "Brodie is shot. Take command of the left in his place."

Back with his men, Roosevelt led on. The country became more open, but they saw no Spaniards. Search with glasses revealed a few red-tiled farm buildings ahead — was the enemy in hiding there? He ordered a charge, but by the time the buildings were taken, the enemy had gone. Only the dead showed the toll paid. But perhaps the Spaniards were hiding somewhere near?

Roosevelt sent out small groups to get information. Before any returned, he impatiently went himself to see what he could learn. Quite by chance, he came upon a group of American officers standing, relaxed, under a tree.

"The battle is over," someone told him.

"You did well," another added, casually.

Roosevelt was so astonished he could not reply. So *that* was war? Acting the best you knew. Risking life without knowledge of any plan or objective — he felt deflated, unhappy.

Later he tried to talk to Davis about it. "A man has to do his best and hope it is right," he said, still puzzled.

There was time to think it over in the week that followed — a week that wore on officers and men. Supplies did not reach them, and they had little food.

Roosevelt spent three hundred dollars, all he had with him, and personally borrowed a hundred dollars more, but it was not enough. The years of revolutionary fighting had depleted the land; cows, poultry, eggs, garden truck, were lacking. The wounded, the sick, got tender care, but many died from lack of shelter and medicine. The regiment's close, friendly feeling, begun in Texas, grew into deep devotion to the unit and to Roosevelt personally, during that time of anxious waiting in Cuba.

During that week, the commander became ill, and in the shift of authority Wood was given a brigade and Roosevelt was made acting colonel in charge of the regiment. He was happy about this in two ways: first that the new responsibility came after the first skirmish that taught him so much; second, that it came before the next fighting.

As the week ended, orders came to attack the forts of Santiago. Troops moved forward and camped at El Poso, near the city. Directly in front of the American troops lay the San Juan hills with their ring of forts. There, tomorrow, the battle would be fought. No preparations had been made for men who were to fight that battle. There was no food. Only a very little artillery had come. There were not even any orders — only rumors.

"Admiral Cervera and the whole Spanish fleet are bottled up in that harbor," someone had heard.

"Our fleet is just outside," another remarked hopefully. "They'll get 'em!"

"How? Spanish forts guard the harbor entrance — we have to take those forts first, you know." The man said no more.

Few slept that night of June thirtieth, 1898. Empty stomachs and the thought of those frowning forts on the hill were not soothing as men waited for the morning.

On San Juan Hill

The battle of San Juan began at dawn with a burst of fire from the fort on the hill. Several Rough Riders were killed or wounded. A Spanish bullet hit Roosevelt on his wrist; it raised a welt but did no other harm.

Surely they should attack — but he had no orders. Then word came to *wait!* Incredible! Rough Riders were directly under the guns of the fort; many lives were lost in that period of waiting.

Roosevelt tried to get an order to attack and end the slaughter. His men were in the lead, ready. The heat was fearful. Grass on which they lay seemed as hot as the devastating flame and shell.

Finally an order came to support the regulars, assault the hill, and take the blockhouse. Here, at last, was a clear objective — hard, but definite.

On his horse, Texas, Roosevelt rode along the line, giving the order. Regulars hesitated, doubting his authority.

"Then let my men pass through!" he shouted. Rough Riders grinned, as they pushed ahead. Many regulars joined in the rush up the hill. Roosevelt rode a hundred feet ahead, his sword high — a stirring leader.

"Forward! Charge!" he shouted in ringing tones. A blue polka-dotted handkerchief tied around his sombrero drifted behind him like a banner. He felt an exhilaration, a kind of happiness. No doubt of his duty troubled him that day. His orders were clear: "Take that hill."

"Forward!" he turned to shout again. The troop followed him. Bullets hissed by. Men fell, rolling over in the grass, screaming. More men took their places. The line went up — and up — creeping, stumbling over the coarse, hot grass.

Incredibly, the leader was not hit. Afterward men said the Spaniards were too astonished to shoot at him. He advanced higher, and felt no fear. The pent-up restraints of boyhood, all his earnest longing to do right, to be courageous in time of test-

ing, drove him onward. A glorious, free feeling spread over him. Bullets? What are the hazards of bullets when a man has a chance to live intensely?

They won the hilltop. The trench fighting lasted but a few minutes. Prisoners were taken, and provisions — food was a special prize. Late in the afternoon the Spaniards attempted a counter-attack, but were easily driven off.

As firing along the hills died down, word came through that other forts had been taken, too.

Weary, hungry men were eager to push on, while they had the advantage, and take the city. Only positive orders to stay where they were prevented them from going forward.

The next day pouring rain turned the earth to mud. Many of the shelterless troops sickened. All were discouraged when a siege, instead of a battle, was ordered. On July 3rd, the United States commander demanded the surrender of Santiago. He threatened to bombard the city with heavy guns if it resisted. Most of those guns were still in Tampa, but the Spaniards did not know that.

The American troops were ignorant of many facts, too. They did not learn until later that while they sat in the mud, laying siege to Santiago, Admiral Cervera, a bold and brave Spaniard, had wearied of lying at anchor in the Bay with the United States Navy standing guard just outside. On July 3rd, his fleet made a daring and orderly dash out of the harbor into the very teeth of the United States fleet. Cervera's chances, as he well knew, were slim. But he hoped at very least to make that enemy fleet pay a high price for taking him.

As the line of Spanish ships came forth, each engaged the nearest ship of the American fleet in a magnificent kind of duel. Smoke, flame, and the terrifying sound of shell crashing on metal decks filled the air. The Spanish powder was poor; their aim unskilled. The American ammunition was excellent and the marksmanship superb. Roosevelt had a glow of thankful pride when, later, he heard that news.

In four hours of brave and terrible fighting the Spanish fleet was lost. Cervera had to scuttle ship after ship upon the sandy shore. Where it was possible, United States ships stood by and rescued the sailors. The Spaniards had about five hundred casualties and nearly eighteen hundred men taken prisoners. On the United States fleet, one man was killed, one wounded, and no ship was seriously damaged.

When Spanish officers at Santiago learned that their proud fleet was lost, the city surrendered.

Then, with the campaign about ended, Colonel Wood was made brigadier-general and Roosevelt was promoted to colonel and given command of a brigade. He promptly recommended five of his officers for promotion and this was done. Later someone noticed that of the five, two were Catholics, two Protestants, and one a Jew.

"Did you know that, Colonel?" he was asked.

"Certainly. And I knew they were brave, competent men. We served together as brothers."

Immediately after San Juan Hill was taken, the hundred and more war correspondents began telegraphing home dramatic accounts of that engagement. Richard Harding Davis wrote an eye-witness account of the Rough Riders' action that was read and reread across the nation. Part of his story said:

"On the open hillside there was no protection; bullets rained down; shot and shell from the batteries roared . . .

"Then came the order, 'Forward! Charge!' Lieutenant-Colonel Roosevelt led, waving his sword. In the open, men went up the hill. Death seemed certain. . . . Up, up they went with colored troops alongside of them, not a man flinching. . . . The Rough Riders acted like veterans. It was an inspiring sight — and an awful one."

Newspapers carried pictures, fanciful drawings and factual photographs, showing that charge. Americans wore out those papers, reading the stories. The battle was reenacted in hundreds of backyards by boys who wore polka-dotted handkerchiefs floating from their hats.

Troops still awaiting transport at Tampa mourned enviously that the war was over too soon.

But the war was not over. Only the battles had ended. In Cuba men lay sick, dying — of wounds and dysentery; of yellow fever and malaria. One-tenth and more of the troops who fought at San Juan died; thousands more were to die of malnutrition, wounds, and disease. Even on the homeland, in camps in southern states, hastily assembled troops died, poisoned by bad food, typhoid, and infected water. The whole tale of inefficiency and graft was a national scandal.

In discussion of all this, many talked bitterly against Colonel Roosevelt. Some blamed him for the war.

"His harping on preparedness stirred up the war!"

"The man's a show-off," they said. "He's after limelight."

Colonel Roosevelt did not hear his critics and would not have cared if he had. He was in Cuba, with the troops. Though these soldiers had served prosperous America, they now lay ill, in tropical heat, and without ordinary comforts.

Lack of food and supplies was mainly due to the failure of transports to co-operate and also to the failure of the army to build or repair docks where supplies could be landed. Men burning with fever from malaria lay unsheltered on the beach in sight of ships laden with needed medicine and food. But no one saw to it that those supplies were brought ashore.

For a few weeks, while the newspaper tales were news,

people talked of the glorious Cuban war. Then, quite suddenly it seemed, citizens turned to other interests. Soldiers dying of malaria were not exciting, like a battle.

But Colonel Roosevelt was with his men. The leader who had gallantly charged up a hill under fire was now transformed into the man his children knew — thoughtful, tender, kind. He went about among the sick, helping where he could, comforting if comfort was all he could give. Men shared his ready laughter, often at himself. He was the good companion of ranching days, undaunted by discomforts and privations. Sick men followed him with tired eyes. Dying men begged him to stay a while.

After a time, Roosevelt's patience ended. Someone, certainly *someone*, should tell the American people the truth about their soldiers in Cuba. Whose duty was it?

A bold volunteer might speak out — he would finish his service in a few weeks. But if an army officer complained — if he told the truth about actual conditions, what would happen to his career? To his whole life work? Small wonder that men who were brave in battle hesitated and hoped that improvement would come someway, somehow.

Roosevelt saw this. He wrote a letter and took it to the commander's tent. The general guessed what that envelope contained, for Roosevelt had asked in vain for supplies his regiment needed.

Now the general looked at the envelope, and at Roosevelt. Without touching it, he waved it aside to a newspaper man who was standing near.

The next day Roosevelt's words were spread on front pages

of American newspapers. Thousands of citizens read with horror what he reported. In the mighty stir that followed, army officers were called on for their views. They combined and wrote a letter which came to be known as the famous "Round Robin letter." In it they told the truth about the Cuban campaign; then all signed. There was safety, time proved, in numbers.

Through these two letters and frank reports from newspaper correspondents, Americans learned that high loss of life was due to poor reconnaissance, poor supply systems, and failure to be ready when war was declared. Many blamed the generals and the government. The more thoughtful knew that blame lay directly at the door of American citizens. Responsibility for government is the cost of freedom.

It was a pity that in the stress of the Cuban campaign Americans forgot to watch the movements in Puerto Rico. Few stories came out because most of the war correspondents were ill in Cuba. Yet winning that island was important if Spain was to be ejected from islands near the United States.

For that campaign, General Miles prepared each move with care; he knew the ground and his troops, most of them volunteers. He took Puerto Rico with a loss of only three men killed and forty wounded.

The Cuban campaign confirmed to Europeans their ideas that Americans cared only for making money; that they were inefficient in war and indifferent about government. They thought that the story of Roosevelt and the Rough Riders was exaggerated.

By September Colonel Roosevelt's letter got action. The army was ordered home. Thousands of sick and wounded were transported to Montauk Point on the tip of Long Island. The change was good for some, but bad for others. For a time the shocking death rate continued. Even so, people knew that Roosevelt had saved thousands of lives by boldly telling the truth.

Sometimes truth makes enemies. Many now said that Roosevelt was a "poor excuse for a soldier" and talked of his insubordination. But the men at Montauk Point loved him. And he was the most popular man in the United States.

In a few weeks the First Volunteer Cavalry was mustered out. Tears glistened behind Roosevelt's spectacles as he bade the men good-by. They had been together only a few weeks as a calendar marks time. But in those weeks they had shared fatigue and hardship, hunger and thirst, sickness and death. From that sharing, friendship was born; they would never forget.

Through the summer and autumn politicians were not blind to Roosevelt's popularity. And they remembered that Americans love to vote for a soldier.

"It will be no surprise to Theodore if we talk about his future in politics," a New Yorker remarked.

"Surprise? Why, man, that's what he went to war for!"

"You're wrong. Theodore doesn't work that way."

"He reads history —"

"Oh, yes, he knows history better than most of us. He knows how Washington, Jackson, and Grant were rewarded. But he never acts by calculated design, not Theodore. Impulse, emotion — that's what moves him. I doubt if the idea of being president some day ever crossed his mind when he volunteered for Cuba. He was stirred about Spain's actions and our unpreparedness — I tell you, I know the man."

But Theodore Roosevelt was not offered the presidency, though many thought he could easily have been elected. 1898 was not the year of a presidential campaign and, if it had been, September was too late for a nomination. The only office open that fall was governor of New York. Roosevelt, more than most, knew the trials of that boss-ridden state.

Would he be willing to run for governor? Someone must go to Montauk Point and ask Colonel Roosevelt that question.

The Colonel Moves Up

The man chosen to call on the Colonel in camp was Lemuel
E. Quigg, a minor politician allied with the powerful Thomas C.
Platt. Roosevelt had known Quigg as a newspaper editor in
Montana, and in the East. Platt had been a United States Con-
gressman from New York in the 1870's; and for a time, while
Roosevelt was in the state assembly, Platt was a United States
Senator from New York. In 1896, he had been re-elected to the
Senate.

Platt was a skillful politician and was powerful both in and out of office. He was intelligent, honest, and jealous of his great power. Men who understood New York politics believed that if a governor was to carry out his plans, he must get along with Thomas C. Platt.

Quigg found the Colonel in his tent and they talked for three hours.

"I don't need to tell you about the conditions in our state," Quigg said. "Nothing has changed in your absence in Cuba. Tammany's Boss Crocker rules the Democrats; Platt runs Republican affairs."

"Now, Quigg," Roosevelt objected, "you can't quite couple Platt with Crocker. Platt sees himself as a good man. He is honest, interested in theology, does not take graft — "

"Granted," Quigg interrupted quickly. "Platt's interest is power; sometimes he does good, sometimes bad. But he runs his party. People are beginning to know him; they have heard about the Erie Canal graft; about the taxes corporations do *not* pay. Voters don't like it. Platt's man, Governor Black, can't be re-elected; Democrats are split over Bryan. Republicans might win — with a popular candidate.

"I like a fight," Roosevelt grinned. "I'd like to be governor of New York. I'd try to be a good one."

"Fine! I'll tell Platt. Frankly, county leaders through the state are pressing for you. He can't ignore them. Yet he's not sure about you. How well will you serve the Republican organization in the state, Colonel?"

Roosevelt gazed thoughtfully beyond his tent. Most of the soldiers were gone, the place looked deserted. He knew this was a moment of decision.

"If I am elected, I shall serve all the people of the state to the best of my ability and my conscience," he said, slowly. "I'll not make quarrels. It is enough to fight evil; one should get along with men."

He paused, and Quigg was silent, waiting.

"When I was a boy, we traveled in Egypt," Roosevelt continued. "There I learned a proverb that I have always remembered: 'Speak softly and carry a big stick, you will go far.' I'll not provoke trouble — but I'll fight hard when I must."

"You will be nominated," Quigg said. "Luck to you."

The nomination came soon after the colonel left camp.

Roosevelt promptly planned a vigorous campaign. To his delight Negroes rallied to support him. They had noticed his kindness and fairness to colored troops who fought alongside Rough Riders at San Juan. He was sorry that many independents, some of them personal friends, were not for him. They thought he had "knuckled down under Platt." Tammany, of course, worked furiously to defeat him.

Meetings were arranged over the state. Roosevelt did more traveling than any candidate for governor had ever attempted. He spoke vigorously; words shot out like bullets from a repeating rifle. He looked his audience in the eye, and they liked him. Many who came, curious to see the famous colonel, stayed to hear about honest government.

These talks were in simple, straightforward words. Years with ranchers had taught Roosevelt that men are interested in what they understand. After meetings, people waited in long lines to shake his hand. He had a word for each, and his amazing memory stored names and faces for a lifetime.

Some, remembering Platt, thought he promised too much.

"You offer the Ten Commandments," Jacob Riis said after a ringing speech on better government. "You have a lot to overcome before you get those working in New York."

"Voters can have the Ten Commandments — if they really want them," Roosevelt retorted. "Not all at once; nor easily. First we have to want them. I mean what I speak, Jake."

"I know you do, Colonel," Riis said softly, his face aglow. "If anyone can improve government, you're that man."

On the morning of the election, Roosevelt and a group of campaign workers were on a train, returning to New York City to vote. As they breakfasted in the diner, the train crossed the Hudson River, turned south — and there in full view was the New York State Capitol, flags flying.

"New York voters are putting you there, today, Colonel," a man across the table said. "You'll have a 100,000 majority."

"After all your hard work, I hope I'll get there," Roosevelt replied. "But I'll be lucky to get in by a 15,000 majority!"

That was a shrewd guess. Roosevelt was elected governor by 18,000 — not much, many thought. But it was a huge victory when one recalled that Tammany, before Roosevelt's nomination, had expected to win by 60,000.

Not long after this, Mr. and Mrs. Roosevelt were enjoying one of their rare and happy evenings at home. He read the news of the day while she did a bit of embroidery or worked on the ever-present pile of mending in her work basket. Suddenly

Roosevelt laid the paper aside and sat erect.

"The hard part lies ahead, Edith," he said earnestly.

"Platt, you mean?" Mrs. Roosevelt asked.

"Oh, Platt, I don't dread him. My concern is the people. I've been 'popular' they tell me. But popularity is short-lived. We've had a stirring campaign; now people will settle down to their own affairs and forget their state. That's the greatest hazard in American government.

"But I shall not let them settle down, Edith. I shall continue to stir them up. That's the only way to make people keep an eye on their elected officers."

His wife smiled and picked up another stocking. The boys got such holes! They were active, like their father.

Senator Platt soon asked Roosevelt for a conference.

"I thought you might like to see the list of names for committee appointments." His voice was casual and friendly.

"I thought the speaker of the house appointed committees," Roosevelt remarked with an air of innocence.

"I haven't chosen the speaker yet," Platt said. "But he will appoint the men I choose. Have you anyone you would like me to consider?"

"I'll give the matter thought," Roosevelt said and turned the talk to other subjects.

One of the important posts he must fill would be Superintendent of Public Works. This officer would have charge of the Erie Canal, the cross-state waterway opened in 1825 and still an important link in transportation. Roosevelt wanted exactly the right man for this position.

In a few days Platt again sent for the Governor-elect, and he responded. Indeed, for the most of their interviews Roosevelt called upon Platt. This was not, as his enemies claimed, an effort to gain favor; Roosevelt went because Platt was old and in poor health while Roosevelt was young — and a gentleman. His going was merely good manners.

"I have a nice surprise for you, Colonel," Platt said as he handed over a telegram. Roosevelt read an acceptance of the office of Superintendent of Public Works!

"I'm sorry," Roosevelt said quickly, "but I can't appoint that man to that office."

"*You* cannot appoint —" Platt was speechless.

"I am truly sorry, for I like the man. I think he would make a fine official in some positions."

Platt hardly heard. His eyes were glazed with anger.

"But not," Roosevelt continued, "for work on the canal. He lives in a city served by the canal. He might, possibly, be tempted to profit by decisions. I think it unwise to put a man where he must choose between personal and public interest; I shall not appoint him."

Platt stormed and sputtered, but Roosevelt was unmoved. Later he appointed that man to a responsible post that was free from conflict of interest. He referred the problem of the canal to a non-partisan commission of engineers and business men to study and advise what should be done.

When the day came to begin his term of office, Roosevelt took the oath in the Assembly Chamber. In his inaugural address he said: "It is not given to any man to see with absolutely clear vision into the future. All that can be done is to face the facts as we find them, to meet each difficulty in practical fashion, and to strive steadily for the betterment both of our civil and social conditions." He pledged that this was to be his aim while governor.

The move to the executive mansion in Albany was exciting for the Roosevelt girls and boys. Father would be at home more than he had been for many months. Each morning they visited in his dressing room; an evening hour was for games and for reading aloud. Tales of strange creatures he had seen in Cuba, huge land crabs, buzzards, the terrible spiders, and war stories were the current favorites.

"Tell us about Fatty," Kermit said one morning.

"I've told you that, Son."

"Yes, and don't skip that part about his name."

"We called that cowboy Fatty," Roosevelt began, smiling, "because he was slim as a rail. He'd come to Cuba to fight. He was following me up San Juan Hill when he stumbled on something soft — "

"It was a man!" Quentin exclaimed, eyes wide.

"Yes, a colored man from one of the regiments with us. Fatty bent down; he saw blood spurting from a throat wound. That man would be dead in two minutes! Fatty thought fast. He couldn't use a tourniquet on a neck. He bent down and pressed his thumb against the wound. The blood stopped.

"Five minutes passed; ten minutes — the soldier opened his eyes. 'Better go on, sir,' he whispered softly.

"Fatty nodded, but he stayed; his thumb pressed hard.

"From up the hill he heard shouting, firing; the battle he had come for was *now* — and he wasn't in it. He almost cried, inside; he wanted so much to be up there with his buddies. But he stayed. The wounded soldier still breathed.

"A long time later, after the battle was over, a medical man happened by. 'You saved this man's life,' he said. He dressed the wound properly. 'You can go now,' he added.

"But Fatty didn't want to meet his buddies; he had missed the battle they had fought. Yet his act was brave, too."

"He might have got killed — up that hill," one of the boys said. Roosevelt shaved his chin thoughtfully before he spoke again. The boys were silent, waiting.

"Yes, he might. We all risked that. But for him it took more courage to stay out of battle than to go into it. Remember, doing what you have to do, whether you like it or not — that's courage. Fatty had it, and we loved him."

The boys were silent, thinking over the tale and their father's words. Suddenly Kermit jumped up.

"My white mice!" he exclaimed. "They'll be hungry!" He darted off down the hall.

Roosevelt's eyes followed him fondly. All his children liked pets; but Kermit had a deep, abiding interest in animals. Perhaps he was more like his father than any of the others.

"Thanks for the story," Ted said, as they hurried off. Roosevelt smiled as he went to his desk; he too had a full day ahead.

One of his early interviews was with a group of labor leaders. He had invited them to study with him the labor laws already on the books.

"I thought if we looked them over together," he said, "you could advise if they are fair. And are they enforced? If we need more legislation, let's ask for it. If we have enough, let's see that it is obeyed. I count on your help."

A tenement-house bill came up again, somewhat like the one he had tried to get passed years earlier.

"I think I could put more vim and vigor into this fight if I went down there and saw things for myself," Roosevelt said to Jacob Riis. As it happened their visit was on one of the hottest

days of the summer. They inspected twenty five-story tenements
from roof to cellar. He got ample evidence needed to push
through a new law against "sweat shops" — really workshops in
crowded flats. In his message to the legislature, he demanded
laws to insure better living conditions in tenement districts. In
so far as law could help, the governor intended that it should
do so.

In his two-year term he made economies in government,
improved both tax and civil service laws; got road improvements
that bicyclists needed and saw a good start on new laws to conserve forests, fish, and game.

At that time, conservation was a new field for lawmakers.
Only a man with Theodore Roosevelt's special knowledge and
enthusiasm coupled with his gift for publicity could have
aroused interest as he did. He was aided by a new friend, Gifford Pinchot, who also had unusual training.

Pinchot had been educated as a forester in Europe; he returned to his own country and became the first professional
forester in America. He served in the Forestry Section of the
U.S. Department of Agriculture from 1898 to 1910. Those two
men, Roosevelt and Pinchot, were pioneers in showing the country the value of its natural resources.

New York State's natural wealth was not recognized when
Roosevelt began his efforts to conserve that treasure for the
people. He coined a phrase, "A live deer will attract more money
than a carcass," that helped to save sections of the Adirondack
and Catskill mountains for recreational use.

Platt grew disturbed over the tales of Roosevelt's successes.

The elections of 1900 were drawing near. He called a private caucus.

"We must consider a successor to Governor Roosevelt," he said. "I cannot put up with the man's independence!"

"Successor!" half a dozen voices exclaimed. "The people like him. You can't put him out, Platt."

"No? But we might move him up," Platt said slyly. "Of course McKinley will be nominated to succeed himself, but the death of Vice-President Hobart leaves that office open — "

"You mean make our Teddy vice-president? How he will hate that quiet life!"

"But if the call comes from the people," Platt said, "what can he do but take it?" Gleefully they began to plan.

The Midnight Ride

The moment Roosevelt heard of the plan to nominate him for vice-president he said, "No!" very firmly.

"But T.R. — " a friend protested.

"No, I say! What would I *do* as vice-president? Preside over the Senate? I am not skilled in laws of procedure. I want to be governor again, if the people of New York will have me."

"Could you have your eye on the presidency?" a few were bold enough to ask.

"Certainly not. I am for re-electing McKinley."

"Then we'll look ahead to 1904," friends over the nation began to suggest. "A governor of New York always has a good chance at nomination for president."

Roosevelt valued loyal support given to him and the idea of being president naturally was attractive. But vice-president — that dull job!

However, Platt and his followers had decided. This was the best possible way to appear to promote a popular man while actually getting him out of their state. They cleverly joined with a real Roosevelt boom growing in the West — Roosevelt could not stop them. In Philadelphia that June the Republicans nominated McKinley and Roosevelt. Later Democrats nominated Bryan and Adlai Stevenson of Illinois. And the battle began.

In the custom of the time, McKinley did little campaigning. Success in November depended upon his teammate.

Now that the matter was settled Roosevelt threw himself into this unwanted task with his usual enthusiasm. "Use me any way you like!" he told the campaign manager. "I'm as strong as a bull moose!"

He campaigned for "The Full Dinner Pail," the popular slogan for prosperity — many pails had not been full in recent years. He urged Americans to spread the benefits of industry and civilization. Crowds that flocked to see Roosevelt stood spellbound by the rush of earnest words. He had a direct way of talking; he seemed to speak personally to each hearer. His pointing forefinger, his fist pounding his left palm, got attention. His vigor and honesty won support.

Never in American history had there been such a campaign! He traveled more than 21,000 miles making some 700 speeches to more than 3 million people. The Republican ticket won 272 out of 427 electoral votes cast.

Even Roosevelt's great strength wearied in the long struggle. He went home and rested briefly; then took up his unfinished task as governor. He hoped to complete many of his projects before he had to leave.

By March 4, 1901, the Roosevelts were again living in Washington. Without fanfare, as is the way of American vice-presidents, he took the oath of office and, standing near the President, he returned salutes of Rough Riders who were in the parade. One swung a lasso and roped Roosevelt — smiling, he waved, and freed himself.

That evening, at the Inaugural Ball, people admired Mrs. Roosevelt's gracious beauty. Eighteen-year-old Alice, in white mull, was a picture of girlish charm. Roosevelt knew by name countless people who surrounded him, eager to congratulate him on his new office.

Almost immediately panic enveloped the vice-president — perhaps the only real panic he ever felt. What was he to *do?* Nothing challenged him; no duty roused his spirit. He received delegations and fulfilled countless minor obligations. In May he opened a great Pan-American Exposition in Buffalo and announced that the president would speak there in September. Such duties seemed trifling.

Perhaps he should do more writing; but he had written steadily while doing other heavy work. Perhaps he could now, belatedly, finish the study of law. He asked a Justice of the Supreme Court about this and the judge was shocked.

"The vice-president of the United States go to law school? Surely, my dear Theodore, that is not suitable?"

"Perhaps not," Roosevelt sighed and turned away. A hard gallop in Rock Creek Park might clear his brain and suggest something both interesting and feasible. Of course he had family joys, but those were a man's pleasure, not his work. Luckily, summer was coming.

Sixteen cousins, about the same age as the young Roosevelts, summered at three homes by Oyster Bay. They swam, sailed, rowed; they tramped and played strenuous "follow the leader" over fields and through woods. They rode horses and drove carts and went on countless picnics.

The Vice-President arranged his speeches and writing so that he could often join them. He was as vigorous and active as anyone, and very happy.

In the late summer the Roosevelts were invited to visit friends at a camp near Mount Marcy in upper New York state. Delightful plans included camping trips and mountain climbing.

On the sixth of September McKinley was in Buffalo to speak at the exposition. That same day Roosevelt was guest at the annual picnic of the Vermont Fish and Game League.

The Vice-President's address on conservation was ended and the picnic dinner was over when a message, relayed by private telephones, arrived for him. A man brought it from the house to the picnic grounds.

Guests saw that Roosevelt was moved as he read it.

"The President has been shot by a Polish anarchist," he told the man next to him. "I must put through a call for more information." He hurried to the house.

After quite a wait, word came that the wounds were not fatal; the President was doing well. Roosevelt went outside and made this reassuring announcement to departing guests.

"Now I must leave for Buffalo at once," he decided.

"Buffalo?" A few eyebrows were raised at that.

"Wouldn't it be more seemly if you went to Washington? Or, perhaps, to Oyster Bay?"

"Certainly not!" Roosevelt was not self-conscious. "The President is my friend. I may be of some service. If you will be good enough to get me across the lake — ?"

He left immediately and down the line caught a special train for Buffalo. The news there was good. Three days later, doctors announced that the President was out of danger. So Roosevelt left to join his family in the mountains and take them back to Oyster Bay.

There had been a bad storm while he was away. The roads were dangerous and repairs would take a few days.

"Let's stay here over the weekend," he proposed impulsively. "We can camp in the cabins by Lake Tear-of-the-Clouds and the next day the boys and I can climb Mount Marcy."

As soon as guides and provisions could be arranged the party set out on foot through the forest. Last minute word from Buffalo was reassuring; everyone felt gay and happy.

The five-mile hike, the night in the cabins, and camp breakfast were delightful. Then Mrs. Roosevelt and the younger children started back. The men and boys began their climb up the mountain.

They reached the top and were returning when Roosevelt saw a woodsman running toward him. Instantly, with intuition that seldom failed him, he knew the man brought bad news from Buffalo. The message was written in a woodsman's scrawl, taken down as it was relayed by private telephone from a telegraph office miles away.

"Buffalo NY Hon T Roosevelt," he read, "the President appears to be dying and members of the cabinet in Buffalo think you should lose no time in coming. Elihu Root." Root was McKinley's friend and Secretary of War.

For a moment Roosevelt stared at the paper, silent. Then he told the news and added, "I must get down at once. There will be many arrangements to make for the journey."

It was midnight when Roosevelt tossed his hastily packed bag into a mountain rig and took his place beside Mike Cronin, the best driver in the neighborhood. Through black darkness, over roads washed out by the recent storm, the horses dashed. Roosevelt, silent and thoughtful, clutched the seat arm and his hat; his head was sunk into his turned-up collar. He knew the road ahead — it had been difficult enough in daylight. Mike Cronin did not speak, either. The team needed all his attention.

At three A.M. rain was pouring down. They stopped for a relay of horses that Mike had arranged. At the house a man handed Mike an envelope.

"I took it down by telephone," he said.

"Time for this later." Mike thrust the paper into his pocket. In a minute they were on their way, plunging through blackness. Roosevelt held on, praying.

The eastern sky was gray when the mud-splashed team pulled up at North Creek station. A train was waiting there, steam up, ready. Stiffly, Roosevelt climbed down.

Mike handed him the crumpled message. He tore it open and read:

THE PRESIDENT DIED AT 2.15 THIS MORNING. JOHN HAY,
SECRETARY OF STATE.

The paper slipped from numb fingers, Roosevelt bent down, picked it up, and without a word stepped onto the waiting train. In a moment he was speeding to his destiny.

For hours the country was without a president. Then, in the home of a lawyer friend of Roosevelt, men of state assembled with a judge of the United States District Court. In that library, Theodore Roosevelt was sworn in as the twenty-sixth president of the United States of America.

The new President was the youngest man to take that office — forty-three years old. The very vigor of his personality and opinions gave him ardent friends and bitter foes. What would he do for the country? The cabinet men, all much older, eyed his solemn face and wondered.

The new President was speaking, ". . . the administration of government will not falter in spite of this terrible blow. It shall be my aim to continue the policy of President McKinley for the peace, the prosperity, and the honor of our beloved country." He begged the cabinet members to stay with him — "I shall need you."

In a few hours the funeral train, bearing the living and the dead, was on its way to Washington. Roosevelt was quiet on that journey; perhaps he was thinking of what he hoped to do for the country he loved.

What was that country like in the year 1901?

Many Americans lived a comfortable life; some had great wealth. Most skilled workers could earn a living.

The rich had palatial city houses and elegant country

homes. They traveled, bought works of art, fine clothes and furniture, and entertained lavishly. Many who were not rich were able to live in spacious homes, had at least one carriage, gave parties, sent sons and sometimes a daughter to college. They traveled, though few "went abroad"; they vacationed at the seashore or mountains.

In the whole land there were only about 14,000 automobiles, playthings of the idle rich. People rode or drove horses. Goods went to trains or ships in great horse-drawn carts. A fire engine, its brass shining, was pulled by three splendid horses. Boys and girls ran to see the engine go by — smoke pouring from the stack, the fireman stoking to get up steam in time to pump water on the fire.

A few men talked about flying but no one had succeeded in actual flight. An Italian named Marconi thought he could send messages without a wire. He had succeeded over short distances and was experimenting with oversea wireless messages.

Most sports were still of the frontier sort — camping, fish-ing, hunting, riding. Bicycles were in common use, and brave youths dared long cross-country tours in spite of bad roads. Feminine riders wore short skirts — ten or twelve inches from the ground, at a time when fashion required dresses that literally swept the floors.

Baseball was played on vacant lots; lawn tennis and croquet in back yards, and football at schools and colleges. Two new games were attracting players. Basketball was enjoyed in YMCA gymnasiums and in some schools. And golf had been brought over from Scotland. Some country clubs had laid out links by 1900, and a few cities had public links. People generally laughed at the Scottish game. "What's the fun of chasing a pill around a pasture?" was a common query, certain to get a chuckle.

All that was for the prosperous. Many unskilled workers had been thrown out of work in the depression and found it hard to get a fresh start. The trickle of immigration that began when America was discovered, had grown into a flood. In 1900 nearly half a million came; seven years later, two and a half times that number came in one year. Few in the United States realized that these millions were weaving close new ties between the old world and the new.

These were fine, sturdy people, drawn westward by a hope of freedom and better living. They brought little money, or knowledge of the new language and ways. Many who lacked friends to advise them settled in city slums. There were not enough jobs to go around, not nearly enough; very soon poverty and misery in cities became appalling.

Here and there people like Jane Addams, Lillian Wald, Jacob Riis had a concern for the city poor — but such were relatively few. This was surprising because Americans were naturally warm-hearted and generous. They carried baskets to the sick and poor; they helped neighbors in distress.

Roosevelt knew from his own experience that city slums seemed remote, something read of in a newspaper, perhaps, but not really known or understood. His efforts to make tenements better and factories safer were not really new; but because of his skillful publicity, they were among the first to get popular attention.

The American Federation of Labor had been organized in 1885 and with Samuel Gompers as president worked for standard working hours and wages and collective bargaining. This last was vitally important for with so many wanting each job the man who objected to anything was fired. Wages got so low that workers almost starved. Children toiled in factories or at home.

Public lands out West had once offered a family a chance to make a new start. But by 1900 those were filled. Moving away was no longer feasible. If a man was a factory-worker, he did not own his tools; he did not know farming nor did he care to learn. He felt trapped in dire poverty.

All this time industrial and business power was growing. Rockefeller in oil, Carnegie in steel, Morgan in banking, were a few of the many leaders who had gained wealth and power. Most of these were good men personally, but they thought of workers, not as people, or even as customers, but as "labor" which they bought as cheaply as possible.

The power of the Federal government was growing, too. Washington, Jefferson, even Lincoln, would have been astonished at the vast power now laid upon new shoulders. No wonder that as citizens followed news reports from that train they wondered what kind of a man had become president of their country.

Theodore Roosevelt, now forty-three, had been disciplined by his long struggle for health, and educated more by wide reading than by formal schooling. Travel had early trained him to be with people of other countries, beliefs, and tongues. His life in the West had hardened his body and increased his understanding of many kinds of people. His boyhood love of nature had grown steadily and gave him a unique comprehension of the importance of his country's natural wealth. Jacob Riis and his own warm heart had acquainted him with the hardships of the poor and needy.

Interest in government, begun in a vain attempt to study law, had been turned by Joe Murray into a life work. No one had guessed that the young ward politician of 1881 would come to be a state legislator, a federal officer, a police commissioner. Still less would anyone have supposed that in twenty years this young man would serve in a war, be governor of a great state, and then be president of the nation. Yet few, if any, of the presidents who preceded him, had the wide training for the office that he brought to it.

Strangely, none of his public offices had been deliberately planned for, or sought, by him. He had only been alert, ready — and opportunity had called, even as now, when a tragic death raised him to the highest office in the land.

As he sat silent in that speeding train, he wondered prayer-fully whether he would know how to use the power thrust upon him. Could he make the country a better place for *all* citizens, not just a few? Like countless Americans he, too, wondered what this sudden change in leadership might mean for the United States of America.

President Theodore Roosevelt

Americans got their first real information about their new President's intentions when they read his message to Congress in November, 1901. He had written it himself and, for him, it was a cautious paper. Many readers thought it was the most personal state document since Lincoln's time. The President had had it printed — a new idea.

Newspapers reported that members of the Congress had listened to it with rapt attention. From the first sentence, announcing McKinley's death, to the last, expressing hope for world peace, the reading took two hours. At the end vigorous applause showed approval. Newspapers spoke of the message as the words of a statesman, not a politician.

The President spoke about trusts, which many thought were a new danger to the nation. The word "trust" as he used it was as new to many Americans as the danger Roosevelt perceived. They were to learn that a trust was a combination of companies — industrial or commercial — which joined together for their mutual advantage. By joint management they could reduce expenses, control production, and defeat competition. These objectives had both good and bad phases; the President told the Congress that he believed trusts should be watched and that the public should be informed about them. He believed that public knowledge was a safeguard, needed in business as well as in government.

Roosevelt asked for laws to provide a lower tariff — but not so low that American labor would be hurt; for a new department of Commerce and Labor with power to watch big businesses and protect workingmen.

The message considered the care of Cuba, Puerto Rico, Hawaii, and the Philippines, the need for a stronger navy, and other issues. The President's frank approval of the traditional Monroe doctrine pleased many who had wondered how he felt about that.

"T. R. is doing all right!" people said with relief.

"It's a sound statement. No need to worry about him."

"He's upsetting no applecarts — but he looks ahead."

Roosevelt himself was pleased, but not deluded.

"Don't be taken in by my popularity," he said to a relative. "It never lasts. I shall be equally unpopular one of these days — and I'll come through that safely, too."

"Yes, if you can keep citizens interested."

"I did while I was governor," Roosevelt smiled. "I'm not the quiet type they can forget."

Newspapermen were fascinated by the fresh aspect he gave to public relations. New stories appeared daily.

"Look at this!" a woman reader exclaimed. "The President had company to breakfast! That'll set a new fashion."

"And he sent 'em away so he could get to his office at half-past eight — see? It says so here," her husband added.

"That's a killing pace! Of course the man is young, but he'll get sick. You'll see."

One of the new rules Roosevelt laid down was that he was to have two hours of exercise each day. He rode, walked, boxed or played tennis, always trying to get the most benefit from the shortest period. Evening work more than made up for the two hours taken away from his desk.

Boxing matches had to stop after a chance blow cost the sight of one eye. His pride in perfect health made him keep the accident secret from all but his family.

Tennis was the quickest recreation because courts were on the White House grounds. Several men in the executive department were good players. In time the group became known as the "Tennis Cabinet." It included reporters and visitors — Gifford Pinchot and many Westerners, such as Bill Sewall, played a hard game that delighted the President.

These hours made news for reporters. But Roosevelt was a particular joy for cartoonists. His stalwart figure, eyeglasses, wide-brimmed hat — and of course his friendly grin — made amusing cartoons. Artists sketched in Western backgrounds and put the President in cowboy or Rough Rider outfits, very novel for a national leader. Words on the cartoons were often set down in "simplified spelling," one of his hobbies, and in popular slang. Readers were sometimes misled to think that he spoke in a slangy manner; but when they heard him talk they found he used the excellent English he acquired in boyhood.

The President took this teasing and the stories with laughing good nature and the people admired him the more.

His official cabinet thought him a bit adolescent. But then, he considered them old men! John Hay, the Secretary of State, had been Lincoln's private secretary. Long, still Secretary of the Navy, had been Roosevelt's boss. All were years older than the President and were confirmed in habits of dignity.

Often these statesmen paused in amazement as they met boys and girls racing in White House corridors or playing hide-and-seek. Such shrieks of laughter had not been heard in this mansion since the Lincoln boys indulged in games indoors and accumulated strange pets out-of-doors. Occasionally the President wondered whether citizens would criticize his boisterous games and tramps with his children. But he never wondered long; a father had rights and privileges even though he was the President.

There were quiet hours, too, when he read aloud to his children. When work kept him at the office, Mrs. Roosevelt began the reading and he took over as soon as he could come. Together they read scores of books, at the White House and at Sagamore Hill, where every room had its shelf of favorites.

The first Roosevelt Christmas at the White House was a joyous occasion. Christmas Eve the children hung stockings in their mother's room.

"You are not to waken us too early," Mrs. Roosevelt warned them.

"Oh, *no!*" the boys and girls promised solemnly. But loud knocking wakened the parents from sound sleep. Mr. Roosevelt slipped into a dressing gown and lighted the fire. The children took down stockings and dumped contents onto the bed, greeting each discovery with squeals of delight.

The tree was in the oval room. After dressing they had breakfast, enjoyed the tree and spread presents on tables — one table for each person. Visitors, delicious meals, and a brisk canter made the day happy in the traditional way.

Soon after the beginning of the year, problems piled up for the President. A few sentences in his message to Congress had been little noticed; he meant them as warnings of the storm he saw ahead. He had spoken frankly against "men who seek gain, not by work, but by gambling."

Roosevelt did not disapprove of wealth — though he never tried to get it. But he thought speculation on the stock market was a form of gambling and dangerous to the nation. Now people saw what words in his message had meant.

Late in 1901, a business called The Northern Securities Company was organized with a capital of 400 million dollars. The announced purpose of this company was to buy and sell railroad stocks. But actually, it was a monopoly of western railroads, the first of its kind.

"This is a good thing — it's real progress," many said.

"I'm glad to see the end of fighting between rival railroads," others approved.

"I wonder." Here and there a thoughtful man pondered. "They can have things all their own way now."

Roosevelt believed in progress. But he did not want any one group to get too much power. They might forget that America was for all the people.

In February of 1902, Roosevelt announced that the government was going to sue the Northern Securities Company for "restraint of trade." By this act, early in his term of office, Roosevelt began his effort to keep wealth from getting too much power. Two years later, the Supreme Court astonished many people by deciding that Roosevelt was right.

Later in 1902 a long quarrel between miners and owners in the Pennsylvania coal field flamed in a terrible strike. Men demanded better wages and living conditions.

Miners then worked ten to twelve hours underground for an average annual wage of about $560.00. That meant that many got much less than that sum. They were forced to buy food and clothing in company stores at high prices. Company housing was shocking. Mine work was dangerous, and there were few safety devices. Scores were killed and hurt. Injured men had no rights; and a lawsuit was expensive and hard to win.

A glimmer of hope stirred when the American Federation of Labor was organized, but that hope died in the face of public antagonism to the riots and violence of the 1890's. Late in that decade John Mitchell, a young miner, president of the United Mine Workers, called a strike for a ten per cent raise in wages. Theodore Roosevelt, and others, liked this man. Senator Mark Hanna of Ohio got the strike settled in 1900, with an increase in wages, but no other gains. Quarrels continued.

By the autumn of 1902 violence broke out, and the governor of Pennsylvania called for state troops to bring order.

The President had no legal right to interfere in state affairs. But with a strike so deadly, Roosevelt thought he had a moral duty to act. He called a conference of both sides.

By some magic never revealed, the President kept those angry, bitter men in conference until he won their promise to settle the disputes by arbitration. In two weeks the mines opened, and there was no violence. The board of arbitration gave the miners an increase in pay and some, not all, of their other demands. This, in 1902, was counted as a great victory for the workers.

During this same period a third matter came up to test the new President, this one in the foreign field. The dictator of Venezuela took for himself property of German and English residents in his country. Germany objected and sent the ambassador to Roosevelt. In diplomatic talk he said, "The Kaiser is sending his fleet. He will blockade Venezuela and get back that stolen property."

Roosevelt knew that usually such an act meant war.

"You cannot do that," he told the ambassador. "You would violate the Monroe Doctrine — the American Hemisphere for Americans. If you land forces in South America you will have war."

The ambassador hinted that England was with the Kaiser. Roosevelt shrewdly doubted that England would fight the United States over this matter. "And you know," he remarked boyishly, "we have a big navy." Both knew it was larger than Germany's. Undaunted, the ambassador wrote to the Kaiser that America was a luxury-crazed people and would never fight. So the Kaiser ordered the blockade. Roosevelt promptly sent the United States fleet under Admiral Dewey to the Caribbean. Secret orders told him to shoot if he saw German troops landing. The two fleets cruised around until spring. Then Germany consented to submit the matter to the international court at The Hague.

These three major matters, each so different, showed the American people the kind of man who was their President. They saw he tried diplomacy first; then acted firmly. "Speak softly and carry a big stick." His method made some enemies. But people as a whole liked his firmness.

The first year in the White House revealed that the beautiful old mansion was too small for a large family and the growing national business. Also the building was sadly in need of repair. So a West Wing was built, and offices were moved from the second floor to new quarters. The first floor was now used for state social functions as originally planned and the family could have some degree of privacy upstairs.

The Roosevelt children went to public schools in Washington, in New York, and in the little Cove School at Oyster Bay when they happened to be there during the school year. But in the fall of 1902, it was decided to send Ted — Theodore, Jr. — and Kermit to Groton, a private school for boys. Here they would get preparation for Harvard College and, more important, would be away from Washington where they were marked for too much attention.

When these two, or any others of his family, were away, Mr. Roosevelt wrote frequent letters to them. Some letters were long, some just a few lines. The writing gave him great pleasure. He had the uncommon knack of writing to them as to equals in age. His topics ranged from home happenings, their studies, football, and friends, to the progress of the coal strike. He was as frank and factual as though writing to a cabinet official.

But along with this he contrived to draw them close into the family circle. He mentioned their mother affectionately —

"pretty Mother went along" or "Mother looked beautiful in the blue dress you like." He recalled to the absent son or daughter pleasures they had shared and reported on the health and spirits of horses and pets. Sometimes he made marginal sketches; they cherished these bits.

Very little advice got into those letters. Instead he wrote frankly what he would do about a given problem and then added, "But you must decide. I know I can trust you." Decision was not always what he hoped for, but he kept his word and let the son or daughter work the matter out.

One bit, however, he often advised, when they told their troubles. "I know I can trust you to stand the gaff, play fair, to be a good man to camp out with." This was not preaching. They knew it was his own rule for living.

The boys and girls loved to get his letters and usually replied without being told to write. Father answered letters promptly, they knew, no matter what the cares of state.

Long before Roosevelt became President, he had been interested in the idea of a canal across the Isthmus of Panama. In that spring of 1898, the country needed naval power for the Cuban War. But the *Oregon,* pride of the United States fleet, was in the Pacific. Though she did her best, the hazardous voyage to the Caribbean took seventy-one days. The United States saw then that the oceans bordering her shores should be connected by some shorter route.

President McKinley began planning. At the time of his death it was almost decided to build a canal through Panama, a province of Colombia.

Many details had to be worked out, but by 1903 the project seemed certain to go through. The government agreed to pay the Panama Canal Company, now reorganized, $40,000,000 for its rights and equipment, including the railroad across the Isthmus. The United States also agreed to pay the Colombian government $10,000,000 at once; after nine years, needed for the building, Colombia was to be paid $250,000 each and every year. In return, Colombia was to let the United States have the use of a thirty-mile strip of land with the right to police it and to build on it a canal open to all neutral nations.

The dictator of Colombia informally agreed to accept this contract. But somehow, the matter dragged on. The Congress of Columbia did nothing. American people were disappointed with this inaction.

"Colombia is trying to get more money out of us," some said. "We should use another route."

Talk about running the canal through Nicaragua revived.

People in Panama grew impatient. They had revolted from many dictators during the past fifty years and now cherished the hope that the canal would bring them prosperity.

Engineers told the President that the Panama route was the better so he delayed action, waiting.

"Panama has had so many revolutions! It would be fine if she had one now. We wouldn't have to wait for Colombia, then." Some such remark was made by several who knew all that was going on. One or two even said this to the President but he made no comment.

"I do not consider helping a revolution in Panama," he told

a trusted friend. "Whatever other governments may do, the United States is not underhanded."

"Panama's independence would be convenient, T.R."

"A free Panama would delight me! But I can't say that publicly. It would encourage revolt. That I won't do."

Later that month, October, 1903, word came that Panama was preparing a revolution and that Colombia was sending troops to the Isthmus. Exactly as she had done before in times of revolution, the United States sent ships to insure the safety of Americans and of the railroad on the Isthmus.

On the fourth of November, Panama declared herself free and her own flag floated over the capitol at Panama City. The revolution was without bloodshed, except for one accidental killing of a neutral.

Panama was now a sovereign state, soon recognized by the United States and other nations. Panama and many other nations rejoiced for surely, now, the canal would be built.

In February of 1904 a new canal treaty was signed, this time with free Panama. Actual work on the great undertaking began at once, with every prospect of success. The discovery by Walter Reed's committee of the cause of yellow fever removed one of the great hazards. General Gorgas came from Cuba, where his genius in sanitation had made Reed's discovery a practical success. Gorgas began the same effective work in Panama. At long last the dream of connecting the oceans was to come true.

With such major matters going well, Roosevelt's nomination to succeed himself as president was hardly a surprise. His election in November, 1904, was a "landslide." He won by a majority of two and a half million — the largest ever given to a president up to that time.

The President and his wife and a few friends got the election returns at the White House. As the result became known he turned to her, smiling, and whispered, "My dear, I am no longer the President by accident."

The Strenuous Life

Blue skies and warm breezes greeted the crowds that came for the inauguration. Cowboys and Rough Riders arrived days ahead and took possession of the city. They galloped on stately Pennsylvania Avenue and then tied their horses to lamp posts while people gathered to admire.

On the way to the ceremony crowds shouted greetings to the President. He stood in his carriage and waved his hat gaily. But in the stand before the Capitol he was dignified and serious as he spoke the traditional words:

"I do solemnly swear that I will faithfully execute the Office of President of the United States and will to the best of my ability, preserve, protect and defend the Constitution of the United States."

When the applause died down, Roosevelt read his carefully written address on national preparedness, and social and industrial justice. The breeze carried his words far:

"We wish peace, the peace of justice, of righteousness. We wish it because we think it is right and not because we are afraid. No weak nation that acts manfully and justly shall ever have cause to fear us, and no strong power should be able to single us out for insolent aggression."

"There is no good reason why we should fear the future, but there is every reason why we should face it seriously."

"We have faith that we shall not prove false to the memory of the men of the mighty past. They did their work; they left us the splendid heritage we now enjoy. We have confidence that we shall leave this heritage unwasted and enlarged for our children." He ended with a plea for devotion to the ideals of Washington and Lincoln.

At the informal White House luncheon which followed, Bill Sewall and his family, Will Merrifield, and others from the West mingled with statesmen and diplomats. Then all went to see the parade.

Police estimated that half a million people lined the streets for the three and the half hours it took to pass. West Point and Navy cadets, cowboys with lassos which they used, Rough Riders, Harvard students in black robes, cheered as they passed the reviewing stand.

"Hi, Teddy!" "Luck to you, Colonel!" men shouted. The occasion was gay and colorful.

That evening at the Ball, Mrs. Roosevelt wore a new color, "electric blue," and looked charming. The six Roosevelt children with many of their kith and kin were surrounded by admiring crowds.

A few days after the inauguration, the President and Mrs. Roosevelt went to New York to attend the marriage of his niece, Eleanor Roosevelt, to Franklin Roosevelt, a distant cousin. Eleanor's father, Theodore's brother Elliott, had died some years before and Uncle "Thee" took his place in the wedding ceremony.

That year, 1905, Theodore Roosevelt did his most important work as a statesman. His power, energy, and patience, seemed unlimited. Part of the time his Secretary of War, Taft, was in the Philippines and Secretary of State Hay was absent because of illness that resulted in his death. Roosevelt carried their duties along with his own heavy tasks.

By this year the world was suffering from the prolonged war between Japan and Russia. Japan seemed to be winning but she would not ask for peace; Russia could not. The situation was steadily growing worse.

With skill and patience, Roosevelt gently prodded them

toward peace. He talked with ambassadors; he wrote to the German Kaiser and to King Edward of England. He encouraged Japan to end the war. He listened to Russia. And after months he won their consent to attend a peace conference.

The meeting was held in a famous hotel near Portsmouth, New Hampshire, in the late summer. Roosevelt stayed at Oyster Bay, in constant touch by wire. The *Mayflower* stood by in the Bay, ready to take him to the conference if his actual presence should be needed.

In August the conference deadlocked, Roosevelt boldly sent telegrams, through his ambassadors, to the Czar and to the Mikado, making urgent suggestions. Agreement came on the 29th of August, and the treaty was signed on September 8th.

As this good news spread over the world Roosevelt was deluged with telegrams and letters of warm congratulation. The Czar wrote:

"Accept my congratulations and my warmest thanks."

"I assure you of my grateful appreciation of the distinguished part you have taken in the establishment of peace." This was from the Mikado.

"Am overjoyed; express most sincere congratulations on the great success due to your untiring efforts." This was signed by the Kaiser.

In due time the Nobel Peace Prize was awarded to Roosevelt for his brilliant success as peacemaker.

Another huge task of 1905 was the organizing of men and machines for digging the Panama Canal. Roosevelt had this project, unprecedented in American history, directly under his care. Congress had appointed a Canal Commission of seven men who should "in all matters be subject to the direction and control of the President."

Roosevelt got advice from the best engineers on the type of canal — sea-level, locks, or a combination of the two, and upon the choice of a route. Experts did not agree but he chose the lock type, eighty-five feet above sea-level because cost and time needed for building were less.

"Now we'll see dirt fly!" Roosevelt said, as blueprints, engineers, laborers, sanitary officers, military experts, and tons of machines and tools sailed for the Isthmus.

At this same time work on conservation and irrigation was going forward rapidly.

As soon as Roosevelt became president, even before he had moved into the White House, two men called upon him to interest him in plans for conservation. One visitor was Gifford Pinchot, whom he already knew. The other was Frederick Newell, a man who had a remarkable understanding of his country's resources. He saw that Americans must conserve their forests, save their top soil, and irrigate the deserts. These men were not theorists, but practical, well-informed workers who had careful plans for reorganizing the departments and getting work done.

"The people act as though our resources were unlimited," Newell remarked. "But at the rate our wealth is being drained off into private pockets, it will be gone before they know it."

"We need you, Mr. President," Pinchot said, "to show citizens what their treasures are and how to conserve them. You are the ideal man to do that job."

"I can do it only with you to help me," Roosevelt modestly replied. "Prepare material for me, and I shall bring up this whole matter in my message to Congress in December."

"Count on us for facts," Pinchot promised. "Forest and water are vital problems our country must solve."

On the very day that the message to Congress was read, a group of western senators and representatives met and began work on what they called a Reclamation Bill. Many men, including the President, worked hard to make a just and effective bill. It was named for Senator Newlands because of his vigorous work on it.

The bill was passed and became a law in June of that busy year, 1902. Because of popular demand created in those months, red tape was pushed aside and work was immediately begun in several places. In the four years between 1902 and 1906, twenty-eight projects were begun. Some of the dams in the irrigation work were the highest yet built. More than three million acres would be rescued from desert and thirty thousand farms would be supplied with water.

Scores of other projects moved toward success; labor legislation, pure food and drug laws, interstate commerce laws, were improved. All this was important to Americans.

A reporter chanced to see the President's engagements for one day of this year. "You are wonderful, sir, — "

"Oh, I'm just an ordinary man," Roosevelt interrupted.

"If you are ordinary," the reporter asked, "how do you explain your great popularity?"

"I get things done. Americans like that."

Roosevelt tried to continue the program of daily exercises that kept him fit. Diplomats and reporters who chanced to call might unexpectedly find themselves on the way to Rock Creek Park for a hike. "Come on!" he'd say to them. "You'll like it." Over rough trails, up and down hills, across a creek they panted, trying to keep up with him.

"You don't think he is going to cross *there?*" a frock-coated diplomat asked timorously.

"Oh, yes," a Tennis Cabinet member laughed. "That is T.R.'s favorite trail. But I can take you back to the carriage if you prefer, sir."

"I'll stay with him," the man said gamely, and made it across a swaying plank.

Early in 1906 the President's daughter Alice was married to Congressman Longworth of Cincinnati. Americans were thrilled with the idea of a wedding in the White House. Newspapers devoted pages to descriptions and pictures, and the bride's favorite color, Alice blue, became fashionable.

Late that same year Roosevelt shattered another precedent; he left the country. With Mrs. Roosevelt he sailed on the battleship *Louisiana* for Panama. He inspected the work on the canal and was an honored guest at a great reception in Panama City. There he replied graciously to the official greetings, wished the people of Panama well and added: "Progress and prosperity can come only through the preservation of order and liberty."

The President's message to Congress reporting on this journey broke still another tradition. The document was not only printed, it was illustrated by many photographs, factual evidence of details told in the text.

"Really! This goes too far!" a shocked senator exclaimed when he saw the paper.

Members of the House liked the innovation; they had the paper published so the people could know what the government was doing with men and money.

American people were even more pleased when, later, they learned that Roosevelt's good management reduced public debt by more than ninety million dollars during his time in office.

The President pondered one matter that troubled him.

"Our people have their minds too much on the Atlantic, on Europe. They must realize that the Pacific Ocean borders our shores, too. How about sending the fleet to the Pacific?"

The friend he asked this question was dubious. "Japan may think you are making war. The world may think that."

"They don't suspect us in the Atlantic. I'm for it!"

So in November of 1907, a fleet of sixteen battleships under "Fighting Bob" Evans sailed away, around the Horn and north in the Pacific. To the surprise of many, but not of Roosevelt, this voyage was not considered a "warlike act." Instead the officers and men were royally entertained and relations between nations were strengthened.

Americans followed the fleet by pictures and news reports — San Francisco, New Zealand, Australia, Philippines, China, Japan, and home through the Suez Canal. When the fleet steamed into New York Harbor February 22nd, 1909, she got a royal welcome home.

Many people marveled that Roosevelt could keep well under all his labors. They should have remembered that he was a naturalist, as well as a statesman, and renewed his strength in quiet as well as in vigorous ways.

Breakfast on the south portico at the White House gave him a chance to enjoy laurel in full bloom and the scent of honeysuckle, damp with dew. Cardinals sang in the blooming catalpas and the yellow-throated vireo built a nest near the White House. Such news was written to the children; he knew they, too, were interested.

Years seemed to move rapidly. Soon 1908 came and with it the question, who should be the next president?

"You'll have to run, T.R.," a Western friend said. "You have to finish your conservation work."

"You're the most popular man in America," another dinner guest added. "You must carry through the labor reforms."

"I am pleased that you want me," Roosevelt replied. "But you cannot tempt me. I believe in executive power. I have tried to use mine for the country's good.

"But power is dangerous. For the nation's safety a president must be limited by time. I like the office. I doubt if any president has enjoyed himself so much. But I'll step out at the end of this term." His tone was decisive.

"Who would you name as successor?" Roosevelt was asked.

He paused; it was a question he had pondered long.

"William Howard Taft is my choice," he said. "He's been a good secretary of war, a skillful negotiator in Cuba, a fine governor of the Philippines."

"A Stand-Patter!" someone objected. The term, meaning one who opposes change, came into general use that summer.

"I think you're wrong," Roosevelt said. "Give Taft a chance. I'll keep my hands off."

A plan had been growing in his mind to get out of the country when his term ended. In the busy spring of 1908 it suddenly took definite form.

Carl Akeley, a famous naturalist, was a White House guest; he sat near the President at dinner. Akeley chanced to speak about the strain of political life.

"I'm going to leave it for a year, when I've finished my term," Roosevelt told him. "I need to get close to nature. I've managed to do a little hunting most years, but this is to be a long vacation."

"Where will you go?" Akeley asked, interested.

"Probably Alaska. I have never seen it."

"Alaska!" Akeley was surprised. "Of course you have done fine work settling that boundary. But if I were going away, I'd choose Africa. You'd see novel sights, beautiful country, big game — " For the rest of the evening the President listened and questioned and that night he decided to go to Africa. He began collecting information.

"I'd like to take Kermit with me," he said to his wife a few days later. "Of all the boys he would enjoy the trip the most. But is it fair to him? He might not settle down to college when we come back. I'll put it up to him."

Kermit was thrilled with the idea. "Oh, I would go on with college! I promise you, Father!"

Taft was nominated in June. The campaign lacked some of
the drama of recent seasons, but he was elected by a good
majority. Roosevelt was happy. Surely Taft would continue
cabinet members he had worked with and carry out plans?

This illusion died soon.

"I should have known," Roosevelt admitted to his family.
"Every man has his own objectives, his own methods; that's
natural. I'm glad I shall be away for a long time."

A storm and cold forced inaugural ceremonies indoors on
March 4th, 1909. After Taft was sworn in and had made his
address, Roosevelt wished him well and left for the station. In
a few minutes he was on the train, going home.

Hectic days of final preparation were interrupted by a
luncheon in New York, honoring Roosevelt. Men were interested in his plans and curious about his reasons for going.

"I suppose you find it pleasant to have hunting as a hobby,"
a guest remarked.

"*Hobby!*" Roosevelt was shocked. "My trip has a serious
scientific purpose. Oh, I need a vacation, but I would not stay
away a year for that. I shall get important information about a
little known continent." It might have been the boy, Teedie,
defending his specimens in the bookcase, or the youth on the
deck of the *dehabeah* in Egypt.

The expedition, he explained, intended to get specimens for
the Smithsonian Institution to display. They needed male and
female exhibits of all large game he could get; and of small
mammals, too. The Smithsonian was sending their Mr. Heller,
and other skilled taxidermists, with him. Roosevelt intended to

write, too. He signed a contract for articles on his journey; later these would be published as a book, *African Game Trails*.

"I've been making plans for a year," Roosevelt added. "Camp equipment, guns, ammunition, clothes, all sorts of supplies are aboard ship. We included a small library of pigskin-bound books Kermit and I have selected."

"You're taking *books!*"

"Of course! We couldn't live without books."

The party sailed on the 23rd of March. Thousands of people crowded the dock to shout good wishes. Across the Atlantic, through the Mediterranean, they sailed and down the east coast to Mombosa in East Africa. There the Uganda Railroad took them into the interior.

. A small seat was fastened on the locomotive, above the cowcatcher, and they took turns observing sights on that long train-ride. They saw birds, hyenas, giraffes, rhinoceroses, and countless other sights, such as telegraph poles knocked down by elephants that used the poles to scratch. Back in the car, they heard amazing tales of a rhino that charged a train and a lion that held up a station. The conductor showed the telegram sent out: "Lion fighting station. Help!"

Their safari — a caravan for a hunting party — was awaiting them at Kapiti. "It's so huge!" Roosevelt exclaimed.

"We'll need it all," Mr. Heller assured him. "At home, people look at specimens in a museum, but they do not realize the work required to get them. We have a hundred men, porters, tentmen, beaters to round up game — we need each man. We have tons of supplies — four tons of salt is just one item."

The safari set off in fine style. A man blowing an antelope horn went first; the American flag, aloft, was next. The long caravan headed northeast into the heart of Africa.

Daily Roosevelt wrote his record; incidents of camp life, birds seen, and trees and flowers; the delight of following game trails packed hard through hundreds of years of travel to a favorite water hole. He had sight in only one, not very good, eye, but he observed and interpreted more than any of the party. His shooting was equal to theirs, too.

Roosevelt wrote of killings; these were for one of three reasons, food for the party, specimens for the Museum, or in self-defense. He hated unnecessary or reckless slaughter.

He wrote of songs the natives sang around campfires; of

the courage and kindness of every member of the party; of the habits of wild creatures revealed on the trails.

After months of riding, camping, hunting, and writing, they came to the Nile. Roosevelt pointed out to Kermit scenes of his boyhood journey, little changed. On March 14th, 1910, they met Mrs. Roosevelt and Ethel at Khartoum — all well and the mission accomplished.

Visitors came to call, and some asked hopefully, "Weren't you in any *real* danger?"

"Never!" Roosevelt said firmly.

"There was Mr. Akeley's elephant, you know, Father," Kermit said and turned to the guests. "We'd got our specimens. But Mr. Akeley wanted an elephant that Father had shot. We

couldn't spare one, but by good luck we found a trail and the size animal Mr. Akeley wanted. We came upon the elephant; it charged angrily. Father could have shot from behind a huge anthill, but no; he stepped out boldly. We knew better than to help — anyway, Father got the beast very neatly." Listeners suspected a good deal more than that brief tale revealed.

"Between us we've sent home 512 skins," Roosevelt remarked. "We may keep a dozen. The rest are for museums."

The journey north through Europe was one long fete. Roosevelt the ex-president, naturalist, hunter, was honored as no American had ever been before.

Often he was asked to make formal addresses, as well as shorter talks. Whatever the occasion he voiced American friendliness and American ideals of freedom and of brotherhood. When he spoke at Oxford University in England, one sentence lingered in listeners' minds for thought:

"True liberty shows itself to best advantage in protecting the rights of others, especially of minorities."

And then they came home.

On June 18th, 1910, their ship passed Sandy Hook and steamed into New York Harbor. Scores of tugs, ferries, steamboats, and navy ships were decked with flags. A salute of twenty-one guns boomed over the water as a revenue cutter came out to fetch the Roosevelt party. The mayor greeted them at the Battery and drove them uptown in the mightiest welcome that had ever greeted a returning American.

Rough Riders and Spanish War veterans were the escort of honor through the crowds. People were moved by Roosevelt's foreign honors and proud of his work for his own country. But the warmest feeling was for a great American and a friend.

It was a heart-warming day for a man coming home. But though he was proud, Roosevelt was not vain of that triumph.

"It was beautiful today," he said at home, "but perhaps a little too much. Soon they may be throwing rotten apples at me!"

Bull Moose

Trunks and boxes were not yet unpacked when men came to Sagamore Hill begging Roosevelt to help them in the fall campaign.

"There's a turn away from Taft," devoted followers told him. "We need you! Democrats are working hard to get control of Congress in November."

"But I am out of touch with politics!" Roosevelt exclaimed. "I'm just any American citizen home from a trip."

His visitors roared. "You are the most prominent man in the world — you know that yourself."

"I'll make no promise. Let me catch up with my writing and reading. Let me learn the state of my country."

Those visitors left with a half-promise; he would see them again in two months. But more men came, almost daily.

Roosevelt listened and read. He pieced together bits of news he had heard abroad and found much that distressed him.

The quarrel about tariff was splitting the Republican party. Roosevelt had promised reform downward; he had thought Taft agreed. During the year in Africa, the struggle between Standpatters, conservatives under Taft, and Insurgents, Westerners and Roosevelt men, grew intense. The bill which finally passed, raised the tariff and left bitterness.

There was a fight in the House, too, about the power of the speaker, autocratic Joe Cannon, a Standpatter. But what troubled Roosevelt most was the dismissal of his friend, the devoted public servant, Gifford Pinchot. The forester had quarreled with the Secretary of the Interior about some lands which under Roosevelt had been set aside for the people. Taft sided against Pinchot and dismissed him. Roosevelt felt the incident should have been worked out; Pinchot's discharge seemed a personal affront and a great loss to the nation.

The rift in the Republican party grew so serious that Roosevelt gave active help in the campaign though he was not running for office. In spite of his efforts — foes said because of them — a Democratic Congress was elected. Insurgents begged Roosevelt to run for president in 1912.

"You would not violate your conviction about a third term, T.R.," many said. "The terms are not consecutive."

"Maybe." Roosevelt would make no promise. "Taft has had a lot of trouble, but I'm sure he wants a second term. Any president does. Wait and see how events work out."

In the spring of 1911 Roosevelt accepted an invitation to speak at the opening of the great reservoir at Roosevelt Dam, east of Phoenix in Arizona. This occasion high-lighted the vast reclamation projects undertaken while he was president. It showed Americans and the whole world that the United States government had taken strides in making arid desert into fertile land. The acclaim on that occasion increased Roosevelt's popularity. His natural flair for publicity still turned the spotlight his way.

The Republican party sadly needed favorable attention. Roosevelt was begged to run for nomination as president in 1912, but he made no answer until spring of that year.

"My hat's in the ring!" he announced the news his friends wanted. From that hour, he worked hard for the nomination. He believed that his followers, Progressives they began to call themselves, not Insurgents, would make better laws for industry, labor, and for all the people.

The convention met in June, at Chicago. The city was jammed; the contest bitter. William Taft was a good man; he had the prestige of office and the backing of the Republican "machine." Roosevelt had world-wide fame, a dramatic personality, and a record of notable deeds accomplished.

On the night before the voting Roosevelt gave one of the

most dramatic speeches of his life. He stated clearly the objectives of the progressive portion of the Republican party. He told them that the party of Abraham Lincoln stood at a fork in the road; they must take the right way ahead. Like the Biblical prophet of old, he shouted:

"We stand at Armageddon and we battle for the Lord!"

Men leaped to their feet, shouting. He was carried to a balcony facing Michigan Boulevard. The street was packed

with people, cheering, yelling for him. He raised his hand —
silence fell upon the crowd as he repeated the final phrases of
his indoor address. He paused, watching them thoughtfully.
Had they heard? Had they understood?

Suddenly the crowds surged toward him, yelling approval.
One man in the throng was heard to say, "Nobody wants T.R.
except all the people!"

The next day a ruling on the seating of delegates prevented
certain Roosevelt men from voting. The struggle, almost a tie
at first, ended in Taft's nomination.

Rebellious in defeat, men swarmed to the Roosevelt rooms
and demanded that he form a new party.

"Progressive Republicans must have a voice," they cried.

"You think now that you want me," he told them quietly.
"At the moment you are angry, too bitter to judge wisely.

"Go home and think it over. Talk with your neighbors.
A new party is a serious breach with the past. Do not act hastily.
Early in August I shall return to Chicago. If you feel then as
you do now, meet me and we shall decide what action is best
for our country." He would say no more.

Soon the Democrats nominated for president, Woodrow
Wilson of Princeton University. Wilson had entered politics as
the governor of New Jersey.

During the summer, progressive men pondered. They felt
that America needed a new party, responsive to new needs as
Jefferson, Jackson, and Lincoln had been responsive in their
times. They believed that both major parties were indifferent
to labor, business, conservation, and social problems. They

hoped that a new party would make America into the nation of their dreams.

On August 5, 1912, another convention opened in Chicago; this one had a feeling of dedication. Eighteen women were among the delegates, thus showing approval of woman's suffrage. Convention members and attending crowds sang "Onward Christian Soldiers" and the "Battle Hymn of the Republic." Roosevelt made an inspiring speech; he voiced the demand for government by the people, not by party machine; for better wages, shorter work-hours, and justice for all people.

His nomination, seconded by Jane Addams, was unanimous. Hiram Johnson of California was his running-mate. They named the party "Progressive," but almost at once the nickname given Roosevelt twelve years before — Bull Moose — was commonly used. It was definitely *his* party.

Roosevelt began a vigorous speaking tour; there was no time to lose. People flocked to hear him; to ask him questions.

One day someone asked, "Won't we saddle too much on ourselves, Colonel, in this big social program?"

"We needn't," he answered tersely. "The government must not be abused. I'll tell you my notion. If you see on the road a man who needs help, give it to him. We all need help at times. But if you see a man lying down, not trying to help himself, don't put him on your back. You might have to carry him always." Another time Roosevelt said:

"A true American does what he can, with what he has, where he is. That's the tradition that has made America strong."

One of his many speaking engagements was in Milwaukee.

There a fanatic shot him in the chest. His spectacle case and the folded manuscript for his speech checked the bullet.

"Don't kill the man!" he shouted to the angry crowds. "He's insane! Shooting is an occupational hazard of public life." Calmly he insisted on making his address. He held a hand over his reddening shirt and spoke to the people — not his full address, but a few quiet sentences, thrilling to his hearers.

Actually words were not needed, his courage told more.

Physicians sent for his wife and succeeded in keeping him in a hospital two weeks. He wanted to be up, fighting.

Naturally he was restless; the party needed their leader. The path ahead was new and untried. Many faltered. Traditional party men, both Republicans and Democrats, hesitated to leave an honored party for an unknown. When the popular vote was counted, Taft had nearly three and a half million, Roosevelt over four million. Wilson with six and a quarter million became president.

His friends flocked to see Roosevelt at Oyster Bay. He was still feeling the effects of the shooting.

"People are saying that you split the Republican party and so elected a Democrat," they told him.

"*I* split the party!" Roosevelt's anger had a tinge of sadness. "I? How about the Standpatters who refused to see the problems in today's world? Oh well, history shall decide. We are but men of the moment."

In a discouraged mood, Roosevelt turned to his desk and came across letters he had laid aside, letters inviting him to speak in Brazil and Argentina. Why not accept, take Kermit and then, after the speeches, explore the interior? A wonderful idea! Kermit was engaged to be married but he would not let his father go without him. His understanding fiancée postponed their wedding and travel plans were made.

"I hope you'll not discuss the Monroe Doctrine, Colonel," a friend who knew about the speeches remarked.

"Oh, that doctrine is the subject I'll talk about," Roosevelt grinned impishly. "You know *I* think that North and South America can learn to be brothers. I think they will understand and like what I shall say."

In the fall of 1913 they sailed from New York. Specimens of animal and plant life collected this time were to go to the American Museum of Natural History in New York. Two members of that staff went with the Roosevelts.

Speeches and receptions took weeks of time. The Colonel was honored in Uruguay, Argentina, and Brazil; he met statesmen and scientists who were helpful in planning his journey. At the last minute they persuaded him to go westward and explore the little known River of Doubt.

"Your records will make a valuable addition to knowledge," they assured him. He liked that suggestion.

They went up the Paraguay River, trekked over the great plateau, the watershed of the continent, and came to the River of Doubt. With twenty-two men, including native helpers, and seven canoes, they set out in late February into the jungle. For two months they were lost to civilization.

This continent, they found, was quite different from Africa. They got no big game! Often they were actually short of meat

for food. They had come in the rainy season — good for river
travel but bad for the health of white men. Insects, some very
dangerous, and poisonous snakes, were a constant threat, along
with hostile Indians in occasional primitive villages they passed
on the way.

The greatest hazard was the many dangerous rapids. At
one place canoes were dashed to bits and the party had to wait,
in great discomfort, while new boats were contrived from logs.
The trip that was to have been short lasted two months and
many of the party were ill.

Near the end of the journey Roosevelt was seriously ill with a terrible tropical fever. He lay in a canoe, too weak to hold up his head when — there, before them — the river suddenly dropped into a deep canyon between high cliffs. Surely no frail canoes could live in those tumbling, rampant waters!

Roosevelt heard the roar and rightly guessed the danger ahead. He motioned Kermit to come near.

"Go on, Son," he whispered. "I can't make it, and I won't hold you back."

Shocked, Kermit stared at his father. Never before had that courageous man given up — he was nearer death than Kermit had guessed. Something must be done quickly.

Roosevelt was got ashore, put on a litter and carried ahead, over the cliff. The others began the terrifying task of getting canoes and men through. Afterward they hardly remembered how they managed to rope themselves together, climb the jagged, slippery path and drag behind them those canoes. The full details of that superhuman effort were never told. Perhaps the men wanted to forget the torrential waters, the mighty rocks, the roaring sounds that beat upon their ears!

But somehow, the incredible feat was accomplished. In quiet waters below the rapids, Roosevelt was laid again in a canoe and the party floated safely on — to the Amazon, to the city of Manaos. Somehow he gathered his strength and lived to board a ship for New York, and home.

Kermit left at once for Spain and his marriage to the daughter of the American ambassador there. As Roosevelt's strength gradually returned, he worked quietly, at Sagamore Hill, getting his notes and diary in shape for publication. The book was called

Through The Brazilian Wilderness. Along with his work on the book, Roosevelt wrote monthly articles for the *Outlook*, a magazine that approved his progressive ideas.

Then came August, 1914. Germany invaded Belgium and so started the First World War. President Wilson asked Americans to be neutral in word and thought.

"The President must have information that he cannot tell us," Roosevelt said and tried to obey. For himself, the issue was clear from the first minute; the civilized nations should not allow Germany to crush a little country.

"How can a man be *neutral* in a question between right and wrong?" Roosevelt asked his intimate friends — and got no answer. So, after a time of waiting, he began to write articles begging Americans to prepare for war. With a nation running wild, like a madman, getting ready for action was simple common sense, he wrote. But the administration at Washington had a different point of view.

In January of 1915, at a Harvard Club dinner, someone asked General Leonard Wood if he couldn't do something toward training men for service. Roosevelt, and others there, quickly took up the suggestion. Their first move was to start a list of men who had skills and would serve their country. By February thousands of telegraph and telephone operators, bridge builders, mechanics and such, were registered.

In May, Germany sank the S.S. *Lusitania* with a loss of over a hundred American lives. Immediately General Wood was swamped with letters from men who wanted training for military service.

That summer he opened the first officers' training camp at Plattsburg, New York. More than twelve hundred men registered. They paid their own expenses; they sweated through drills in the daytime; they studied late each night, for five weeks. It was as mixed a group as gathered with Roosevelt seventeen years earlier, at San Antonio. Roosevelt and his four sons were there along with lawyers, businessmen, artists, policemen, farmers, sportsmen — drawn together by a flaming eagerness to serve their country.

The next summer business firms contributed large sums; thousands of men registered and the training went on. By the next year the government took over the camp; it had proved its value, and the men trained there were needed. Such camps became accepted as part of the American military system.

In November of 1916, Woodrow Wilson was re-elected president on the slogan, "He kept us out of war." But during the winter public opinion changed rapidly. In February, diplomatic relations with Germany were broken off and in April, Congress declared war against Germany.

During these months Roosevelt had been receiving thousands of letters begging him to join with the Allies and to accept volunteers to serve under him. So, after war was declared, he personally called upon the President and asked permission to raise and equip a division for service in Europe. More than three hundred thousand men were waiting to enlist under Roosevelt. Many Europeans, too, wrote urging Roosevelt to come — and quickly.

The President refused his permission. At once, Clemen-

ceau, premier of France, wrote to President Wilson asking that
he allow Roosevelt to come. "His name is legendary in our
country," the premier wrote. "He is imbued with simple, vital
idealism. His coming would cheer the Allies." But to no avail.

Roosevelt was saddened, but not crushed. Refused a sword,
he labored hard with his pen. For months his was the strongest
voice in America, prodding a pacifist Secretary of War to prepare for a war already declared. Roosevelt's four sons and a
son-in-law, Ethel's husband, Richard Derby, enlisted and were
in active service.

Over the years since the Brazilian journey, Roosevelt had
suffered occasional returns of that tropical fever that had laid
him so low. In February of 1918, he had a very serious attack,
with abscesses on his legs and in his ears; he was in a hospital for
a month but seemed to recover, though he lost the hearing in
one ear. On his return home, he continued speaking and writing.

On a hot July day when Roosevelt was leaving Sagamore
Hill to speak at a large meeting, word came that Quentin had
been shot down in France. Quentin, their aviator, their youngest was dead!

"*I* should have been the one to go," Roosevelt said sadly.
"*I* should be fighting!" For in that war, men felt that they were
making the world permanently safe for all free peoples. Since
he was not to fight, he did now his nearest duty — went on and
made the speech he had promised.

His earnest, strenuous work, combined with his concern
about the state of the world and his personal sorrow, affected his
health. On the day the Armistice was declared, soon after his

sixtieth birthday, he was ill again and in the hospital for some weeks. He came home to Sagamore Hill on Christmas Day, cheerful and happy to be in that place he loved so dearly. He planned new writing, enjoyed his children and grandchildren with his usual cheerful optimism. Illness, loss of half his sight and hearing, sorrow, disappointment — none of this could defeat Theodore Roosevelt.

But he was not as well as he had hoped. Death came in his sleep, before dawn of January 6, 1919.

As the great leader passed from the scene some people remarked sadly that his last years were an anti-climax to the heroic earlier period. That view misses the point of his life. He always did what was needed at a given moment. In that confused pre-war and early-war era, the pen of Theodore Roosevelt told Americans and the world that ideals of freedom and justice were not dead; gave hope that America would help — in time. Perhaps that was the greatest service of his life.

He called himself a politician and so gave dignity to that word. He worked constantly with men whose aims were below his, but he never lowered his own standards. By temperament he was a man of action. Politicians and government made mistakes; they needed criticism. But he knew that progress comes through action, not talk. He believed that each American should join a party and work with men of every race and creed and level of interest for the good of all men.

Theodore Roosevelt's interests were wide. He loved nature and all living things and his knowledge of them was amazing.

He was essentially a simple man. Right was right; wrong was wrong. His actions were direct; always he followed the trail straight to his objective. He had the bigness, the generosity, of a man who knows his own nature and can get along with himself.

His gift for friendship was notable. His memory for names and faces never failed; his handclasp was heartening. Men worked with him as an effective team; and he gave full credit to each one for work well done.

Love of his country, of the ideals which make America unique, dominated Roosevelt. His patriotism moved him to serve in small ways as in the more spectacular. In ward and city, in state and nation, he did his best to bring honor to his country. And when far away, he so conducted himself that he made new friends for the land he loved.

Theodore Roosevelt believed that American ideals point the way to brotherhood and the good life. He thought that this goal would be realized sooner when each citizen recognized his proud heritage and joined the fight for freedom and justice.

Important Years

in the Life of Theodore Roosevelt

1858 — Born October 27, at 28 East 20th Street, New York.

1869 — With family took first trip abroad.

1871 — Began the study of taxidermy.

1872 — The first gun; the first spectacles.

1872-3 — Journey on the Nile, in middle Asia, and Europe.

1876 — Entered Harvard College.

1878 — Father died. Met Alice Lee.

1880 — Graduated from Harvard College. Married Alice Lee.

1881 — First interest in politics along with law studies at Columbia University. Traveled abroad with wife. Completed *Naval History of the War of 1812.* Elected New York State Assembly.

1882 — First book published.

1882-4 — Three terms in New York State Assembly.

1883 — Summer vacation in the Bad Lands of Dakota.

1884 — Sudden deaths of both wife and mother. Built home, Sagamore Hill. Delegate from New York to National Republican Convention.

1884-6 — Ranchman in Dakota.

1885 — Published *Hunting Trips of a Ranchman.*

1886 — Candidate for mayor of New York. Married Edith Kermit Carow in London.

1889-95 — United States Civil Service Commissioner. Published *The Wilderness Hunter,* biographies, and some history.

1895-7 — President of the Police Commission of New York City. Finished four-volume work, *The Winning of the West.*

1897-8 — Assistant Secretary of the Navy.

1898 — Resigned to volunteer for Spanish war service. Became lieutenant colonel in the First United States Volunteer Cavalry (Rough Riders). Battle at Las Guasimas. Battle of San Juan Hill. Elected Governor of New York.

1900 — Nominated for Vice-President of the United States.

1901 — Took office. McKinley shot. Theodore Roosevelt became the 26th President of the United States.

1902 — Brought about laws to restrain trusts; settlement of a strike of coal miners; peaceful end of quarrel between Germany and Venezuela; extensive remodeling of the White House.

1903 — Began negotiations for the Panama Canal. Settled Alaskan boundary dispute.

1904 — Re-elected by a record-breaking majority.

1905 — Awarded the Nobel Peace Prize for his part in negotiating peace between Russia and Japan. Digging on Panama Canal begun. Work on conservation.

1906 — Worked for many new laws: homestead, food and drug, railroad rates, and others.

1907 — Sent United States Fleet on record-breaking voyage around the world.

1909 — Retired from presidency, refusing renomination. Sailed for Africa for big game hunting.

1910 — Honored on trip north through Europe and in England. Published *African Game Trails* and *The New Nationalism*.

1911 — Opening of the reservoir at Roosevelt Dam, Arizona.

1912 — Announced himself a candidate for Republican nomination as president.

1912 — Defeated by William Howard Taft at National Convention. Nominated by new Progressive party. Shot while campaigning in Milwaukee. Defeated by Woodrow Wilson.

1913 — Completed autobiography and other works. Sailed for South America to make speeches and to explore the River of Doubt, afterwards named for him. Became ill in jungle.

1914 — Published *Through the Brazilian Wilderness*. After beginning of World War I, did writing and speaking on behalf of national preparedness.

1915 — In training camp with sons at Plattsburg.

1918 — Son Quentin, an aviator, killed in France.

1919 — Died at his home at Oyster Bay, January 6.